Words
That Rock
Your Soul

BY
Susan
Hill

May you be brought
up in the NAME of the
LORD
May His FACE
Smile on You

Susan Hill
2014

BOOKS
1 and 2

FOREWORD

I am sure you will enjoy this book. This is my second publication. My original book has been expanded with over 40 new poems and artworks.

I have had no formal education in publishing or in artistry but I have tried in words and pictures to give a new start on spirituality and the effects felt by the soul. As you flick through this book, you should be caught by the first few sentences. The contents of this book will move you from laughter to tears, from joy to sorrow, from horror to comfort. I have tried to 'lift up' your emotions with these poems. You will find yourself saying, 'I always thought that. I don't agree with that.'

The poems are a few-seconds glimpse into another world. A world that perhaps you have always wished for. Each poem shows a facet of existence that may have been hidden from you. Most of the poems have stories behind them, how and why they were written. Here are some examples.

'Plaster Saint' on page 16 was written after a trip to the Victoria and Albert Museum in London. After looking at the fabulous Chinese, Japanese and Korean artefacts; I went for a stroll in the museum and saw signs for the 'Plaster Rooms.' I wandered into the exhibit. My mind was assailed by these huge monoliths, apparently made out of stone. I was misled. They were all made out of plaster and were very fragile.

In other words they were 'fakes'. They appeared the same as the real thing! Also the effect of them being close together, and so huge, was very claustrophobic. The feeling of 'fake-ness' stuck with me. I know that as people we can have a 'fake' appearance. Looking and sounding like one thing, but being made with a crumbling surface!

'Mellow Meadow' on page 49 was from a memory when I was a child. I was out playing with my friends, in the 'Rec', recreation ground. The grass was very long and on hot sunny days we would all lie in the grass and listen to the birds, feel the sun and chat quietly to each other. What bliss!

One more story! 'Short span' on page 45 was inspired by another trip to London. It was very hot and crowded in the underground. Quite unpleasant too! I was looking around, nonchalantly then I saw a beautiful butterfly, a wonderful blue colour. It was fluttering in a jumpy, lost way. All of a sudden an underground train came into the station as it settled on the rail to rest. You can guess the ending. I reached home and went into a department store. I could not believe my eyes, because another butterfly came in above the heads of the shoppers and made its merry way, around the store. This was just a short visit. I lost sight of it. On reflection at home I remembered the 'short span' in time that we are given. What will we do in it? How fragile we are? How suddenly it all can end!

I have gained inspiration from many sources. My main source being reading and studying 'The Holy Bible', sermons, incidents, listening and watching how people interact. Even films and TV programmes. I never plan a poem. The influences of the above sometimes has an overwhelming impression on me. I do not even attempt to write about the impression on my soul. I leave it on the back boiler and forget all about it.

Other times I write it down straight-away. I never know when the 'inspiration' will strike.

When it does I usually pray under my breath with the words 'What next Lord!' then the poem is created.

I have written all these works as I was inspired, there were tough ones e.g. Roman Justice, The Lady and the Tramp and Child Within. These were very emotional and they were difficult to write down. This short poem shows the struggle.

Write It Down

Does the Lord want me to write? That is why I cannot sleep.
Has sleep eluded me because I will not obey?
Is the night extended because of words not spoken or written?
Why can I not sleep; why do my eyes refuse to drift and go?
The Lord has something to say; something to hear.
I want to sleep; I want to dream - do not ask me to do this.
It's no use; it's now that He needs my reply, my prayer.
My asking for forgiveness, my silence will not stop Him.
"Come" He says, "Do as I ask - the task is not great -
I have already seen the outcome."
"Close your eyes, but talk to me. Reach My heart as I have reached yours.
Do as I say NOW - do not delay!"
but not NOW - the morning is over the horizon.
Because I have obeyed and listened to Him, I now S L E E P!

The illustrations have stories behind them as well. I would like to wet your appetite and tell you some of them. On page 5 is the picture 'Thundering Hooves'. This depicts the four horses in the Bible that are in the story of the Apocalypse. With such strife in the world today I felt it was apt. But note there is an opening in the clouds. Hope glimpses through. Can you see the fourth horse?

The image on page 27 represents 'Grace'. I wanted to capture in a simple way what grace is like. In a service I asked the Lord, 'what is grace like?' I saw the picture of white roses, unblemished by a dark, dirty background. We are, in the sight of God, unblemished by our dark backgrounds.

The lighthouse see page 39 is not quite as it seems; it represents Jesus Christ. The picture is called 'Mind the Rocks.'

I have also inserted a study guide and bible reference section for your continued pleasure. If you wish to see more of my work, please go to my website; contact details are on the site and information about purchasing artwork also. Details of reviews will also be available.

I hope you enjoy this book. I know that it will stir the soul. I have never been the same since I wrote these poems. I know the same will happen to you!

www.rock-your-soul.co.uk   Susan Hill

CONTENTS

1. What sort of person are you? - Emotions - Character

2. Life's Struggles – Pain – Anger – Where do I fit in?

3. Problems – Puzzles – Passing Time

4. Questions – Statements – Answers

5. Things to ponder – Why? – What? - Who?

6. Reflections – Foundations - Spirituality

7. God's Mind – Character - Emotions

8. God as Man! – Experiencing – Human Life

BOOK TWO
9. The Emotions and Battle continues

10 Eternal Struggles. Eternal life and Eternity

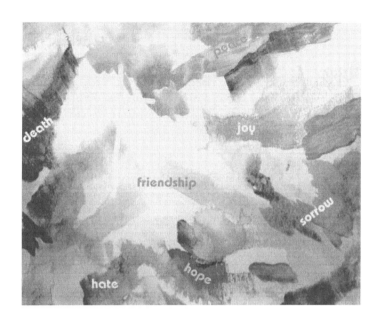

This book is dedicated to all those who seek.
Those who want to change.
Those who know that there is more to life than the physical.

Those who want 'The Eternal' to touch them.
He will. Wait and see.

Child Within

Do not be afraid little one the light will not harm you.
Do not hold back and cower beneath your sorrow and die.
Listen to your Saviour's voice that gently strokes you.
His hand caresses your hiding place wishing to come in.
Do not be afraid little one!

You have heard other voices and screams in the dark.
You do not wish to be alone - but dare not join in.
Some of the shouts are bold and harsh -
and thrash the air -

but the speaker is hurting like you - It is of you!

You want to uncover the pit you are in -
but rocks tumble and hurt.
Your wounds are constantly new - constantly flowing!
Even your heart for release - is so dark and still -
you can't breathe.

You wish you could yell and call for help -
but no noise!
It could never be darker - deeper - or more painful.

The enemy leers and grins and bares his teeth at you.

<u>You are dung!</u>

The smothering continues until no hope remains -
no light at all.
How <u>long</u> you have waited for release - for life.
That scary place!
How you long for newness - but impossibility chokes you.
When you draw back the curtain and speak to the world.
<u>Nobody understands or hears you</u> -
they deny you and go!
Others push pass you in the dark -
roughly handling you -
to reach the air.

A light breaks out!

Bedlam rules so you hide again.
But there is hope. My little one.
A certainty - a life for you!
CALL OUT! For help - reality calls!
Your Saviour rescues you!

Don't Get Wet!

Are you a surface skimmer - too afraid to dive?

Too afraid to plunge beneath the waves.
Duty is strong and straight .
You stand upright - and ride the waves.

Are you a surface skimmer - too proud to fall.

Your face is kept dry and formless words are uttered.
You do not share the sea spray - or the wind with anyone.
Does your day revolve around duties -
and experiences you control.
You stand up when you will - and sleep as you see fit.
You don't move from your position - lest you fall over.
You are rigid and cold inside - but fun is all we see!

Why do you not grasp the wonders - and depths around you?
It's hard to swim - but you forgot you could float.
You can bob to the surface like a cork.
Don't be like a ship in a bottle.
Stretch out your hands - grasp the 'Presence' of the Most High.
Let him carry you over the foam, under the arc of the waves.
Let his breath be hot on your face - let his saltiness strengthen.
Do not be stuck in duty - be struck by him - who is obeyed.

Laugh and be joyful - it's okay to fall off and get wet!
You laugh again and plunge in the depths.
You ride the wind - you scream at the sky.
You have the best companion - the best tide - the best wave!
The best - twists and turns and gets wet.
'LET GO!'

Reflections

The man screamed and raged and people listened.
"Don't talk to them, they are sinners!"
The righteous man cried.
"They smoke pot, have sex and play loud music.
They don't wash - they spit and curse.
They are sinners and lost from God!"

They harkened to his voice, after all he was a holy man.
They not only shut their doors, they shut their hearts.

"KEEP CLEAN, KEEP CLEAN WAS THE CRY!"

The sinful man said, "They don't care about me!
OK, I smoke pot who - wouldn't with the sin around?
OK I have sex and lots of it -
who wouldn't when love has gone to ground.

OK, I play loud music. I dance and bop and prance -
and try to turn my sorrow to joy!
Who wouldn't in a world where nobody cares!"

The gap got wider and wider between the haves and have-nots.
The distance got deeper they were both alone.
They both looked down at each other.
One from pride and the other from pain.

SWAP IT AROUND why don't you?
Help the man in pain obtain pride in who he is - a child of God.

SWAP IT AROUND why don't you!
Let the proud feel the pain of the rejected the lost from God.

Let them both look in the mirror and see a sinner.

Let them both hear the voice of the Healer and Restorer.
Let them both dance a new tune in their hearts.
Feel a real joy in their souls -

AND FEEL TRULY LOVED!

Open Wide

There are many voices in the choir.
Each one singing of its own salvation.
Some are singing with tears in their eyes.
Some can never hear what the sound of their voice is like.

The ones who dream sing in secret.
The ones who paint enrich the words with colour beyond the spectrum.
The players of instruments lift their arms to the skies -
and bring forth music.

The choir is made up of all races - tongues - creeds and voices.
Soprano, bass, treble, tenor - all tones enriched by oil from angel's lips.

The reason that they all sing is because their hearts, souls -
being, spirit, mind, emotions and feelings:
Have all become harmonized by your Spirit.

Your redemption, your love, your joy, your hope, your Spirit and -
the music from your heart!

The heart that beats through the universe is -
the conductor - composer and lyricist -
and it beats the only true tune.

The shepherd of his sheep strums to his people.

THEY ALL CALL BACK THE REFRAIN "AMEN!"

Sound Bites

"What you see is what you get.

Take it or leave it!
What you hear is what you want.
Take it or leave it!
What you do is what you need.
Take it or leave it!

The choice is mine. The die is cast.
You cannot change a leopards spots.
Get yourself sorted! Get a Life!
Get in the mood of the day!
Climb higher – breathe the fresh air of your opinions and life.
Do your own thing!

I am not hurting anyone!
My truth is not your truth.
Truth has no fixed reality.
I plough my own furrow.
Tread my own path. Go my own way.
I'm in charge!
I'm the only reality!

I AM GOD!"

The Lady and the Tramp

"I have nothing!" I said - nothing to spare - nothing in the pot.
"I am skint, my pockets are empty - see only hankies and fluff!"

My pockets were emptied. I was tipped upside down.
An odd coin slipped out and rolled down the drain.
It was of no value. Deleted long ago. - Old coinage.

"I have nothing!" I said. "Nothing - zilch!"

"You must have something!
Something worth selling - bargaining with!"

"I have nothing of value - only yesterday's news -
under my arm."

"That's no use to me!
I need something to sell!
You are a dreamer reading this rubbish."

Her face was close to mine.

"You read this trash, to fill your little life!"

"No!" I stuttered
"My life is very full. Thank you."

Her hands were at my throat, and her breath stank!
She said "Give me something - you old tramp.
You piece of shit! I need a fix!"

Up in the air I went again.
My pockets searched and emptied.
My worldly goods upended.

"You are useless!"

"Please don't kill me, don't cut me.
I'm sorry I'm poor.

I only have one thing that you can't have of mine -
- but you can have of your own!
That's a new life!
Come inside. Have some tea.
The mission's open all day!"

Masque Parade

If we could wear our souls on our faces, what would we be?
Would our laughter lines brighten the day?
Would our sadness and pain etch deep-lines around our eyes?
Would our real feelings to others not flicker and die –
but stay indelibly inked on our faces.
On our mirrored soul?

It would be a terrible thing to behold -
an experience of hell.
Our souls don't wish to be seen.
We hide from the outside world - camouflaged from reality.

Thank God! For the reality of the flesh - it hides everything -
but time catches up on us - our massaged ego slumps!
The reality of the inside <u>does get etched on the outside.</u>
Like a tattoo, sin has many colours and hues.
You cannot find it in an artist's palette.
The dark greys and blacks - greens and reds.
All show up eventually!

The mask is removed.
Removed forever!
Removed in the face of eternity.
Hands gently remove the false face - a hand strokes the cheek.
Tears begin to swell - and well the eyes, washing and cleansing.
The hands stroke under the lids - the edges, windows of souls.
<u>The truth is uncovered!</u>

WHAT DESTRUCTION AWAITS?

Voices

The man that points the way is proud and tall.
He sits on a rock staring in the direction he is going.

He has long words and a shining face kept clean by his hand.

He strides the streets with arrows in his mind;

HE IS GOOD!

The man points the way - the way of truth, but he doesn't live it.
The man grows taller; he shouts the truth.
People cower at his words; they bite the soul.
The man points the way, but no-one follows.

Another man points the way;
He is humble and low.
His voice speaks the truth - also,
He looks into the soul.
He speaks words a child can understand.
He has loves smile.
What a difference - what a show!

The man painted and gaudy.
The man meek and mild.
The man proud of his truth.
The man of truth.
The man whose voice cowers.
The man of few words.
What a difference - what a show!

The first man is any of us - let him point at you!
He believes he is right and sits on the rock.

The quiet man is right.
He has no place with the other.
He is the truth himself.
He has given himself away.
He has humbled himself below the sinner to save him!

THE TRUE 'FIRST MAN'

Heir Apparent

The pain had finished at last -
the child had come into the world.
The father busied himself with useless tasks, not able to cope.
"A boy! Just at this time. A new destiny!"

The mother was tired and strained, exhausted from the birth.
Her eyes rested on the child in her arms.
A treasure a new hope.

"My husband, a child of my womb:
a child of my blood.
Pick up the child and show him to the world!
All the world is his.
See his hands are grasping already!
See his eyes are seeking out the reflected jewels in my ears.

He is just like his father!
Seeking and searching - holding his own!
Just little hands now - but how strong they will become!
See he grasps my robe!"
Then smiles gently and sighs.

"Tell the people he has come.
Tell them a son is born.
The one we sought and waited for has arrived -
healthy and strong.

Tell them Simon!
Tell them - proudly of our son -
our joy!
Tell them we have one to follow the family business.
Who will succeed us?
He will bring wealth to the family!

Tell them Simon about your new son.
The one to be called by your name!
But I won't call him Simon!

I'll call him Judas!

A GOOD NAME DON'T YOU THINK!"

Me Perfect

Words cut deep right into the soul.
People and family do not understand.
Am I meant to be perfect in your sight!
Am I meant to always be under the glory of God!

My heart has pain I wanted to share with the body.
Where is the succour I needed?
Why is pain worse from my friends?
Why do they feel I must be perfect?

There is a knocking in my soul - but I won't let them in!
There is a drumming, a beat in my heart,
I will not listen to.
It gets gentler and gentler less intrusive.
I still feel it!
I am still hurt from the pain!

The knocking continues then a gentle voice.
"May I come in?
May I be with you?
May I sit with you?"

'Who is it? Is it - another who will judge me?'

"NO!" It's a servant of the Lord.
It is one who cares.
One who knows that we all have hidden pain in joy.

It has a gentle voice and touch of someone I know.
It speaks as a friend, someone who suffers also.
It is the servant king the 'suffering one'-
in the form of a human companion of the Way.

IT IS THE LIGHT OF JESUS IN THE SHAPE OF A FRIEND.

Closeness

I dare not look in your eyes and yet I want to be close.
Nearness to you is painful, not because of you but - because!

I dare not speak too loud to break the silence.
I dare not move - in-case I move away.
This is the silent time, the closest time, the most painful time.

I hear words from you that are not even uttered.
Words of comfort, companionship - grief about the pain.

I hear sweet words with no sound because they come from you.

I dare not look in your eyes because you will see MY PAIN.
I will see MY PAIN in your eyes!

I cannot offer it up to you.
It is in my mind.
Too much of a sacrifice for you.
How can I give it to you?

The silence is like a silver light touching my soul.
You cannot take away the pain yet,
IT IS NOT TIME,
but I am comforted.
I don't wish to move away - "Let me stay!" - I cry.

"Of course!"
Says your heart.
"I am always listening.
I have come from the centre of heaven and meet you -
right here, right in your soul."

The pain does not subside -
but I am comforted by your 'Presence'.
It's a joy even pain cannot squash.
What a pleasure, what a joy, what a meeting.

You don't move, you stay as long as I wish.
You have given up your needs for mine.
You listen and speak sacrificially but so gently.

I hear the hum of the world pulling me back -
but I have been in your company.

I HAVE BEEN WITH YOU!

The Meeting

I walked into the room full of strangers.
My heart was pounding as I drew close to you.
Do you see me.
Do you recognise me.
Am I a face you know?
I get very close and you looked at me with that look -
I had always seen.

My hands shook as I opened the bottle and poured -
the perfume over your head.

My soul was released as I watched your face.
MY UNDERSTANDING WAS COMPLETE!

Strong hands grabbed my wrists and angry -
voices shouted at me at what I'd done.

I swallowed anxiously and looked at you.
My gaze was met with thanks and overwhelming love.

I tried to pull away from the strong arms.

At a glance and a word from you - they let go of me.

I stopped the bottle and clutched it to myself.
My tears were now running down my face for you.

I turned to go home happy in my heart and at peace.
I expect the people around me don't understand you -
or what you are about to do!

I look at them as I leave the room.
My family and life waits outside this place.
I look once more at you with pleading in my eyes.

CAN I GO HOME NOW?

Life's Solution.

People weep in the bible, from the beginning of time to the end.
Hearts have been broken!
The plight of Joseph in that jail, do you think he did not feel!
Scream out, against injustice!
This was not the first time for him!

The heart cry of David; when he knew -
he would lose his first born of Bathsheba.
The tears and pain were real, and broke the heavens.
God did not abandon these broken people.
Broken by circumstance. Broken by their choice to sin.
They were not forgotten in the darkness -
and loneliness.

TAKE A STEP BACK, to when your heart broke -
and nobody picked it up!
Have you covered it over with other problems, and other fantasies?
The pain is still hidden deep inside -
unrecognized by you anymore.

TAKE A STEP BACK, you will not fall or die -
even though you think you will.
The pain comes back many times worse than expected –
but you are ready.
Your hands are bleeding with your pain –
inflicted by others and yourself.
How do you wash it off?

What can possibly replace it or heal it?
What can be done to hide it again? You wish you could do that.

Take courage and hope, a greater sacrifice -
greater pain has met and identified himself with you.
Not with the outside you -
but the INSIDE AS WELL!

Do not be afraid! Fear is a killer and destroys!
What you feel, what you hide from,
has all - been empathized by him.
He feels everything, you don't!
The sacrifice was by the son of Mary - Jesus, and Saviour -
brother and deliverer.
HE WILL GIVE YOUR LIFE BACK TO YOU - AND NOT DEATH!

14

The Invitation

It fell on the mat with a delightful plop.
Addressed in copper-plate just for me.
'First Class' delivery on the front - fully franked and stamped.
I opened it excitedly - tearing off the envelope.

'You are cordially invited to a party.'
What joy so 'deserved. - Just what I needed!'

The party frock was pressed, hair primped, make-up on.

I LOOKED PERFECTION ITSELF.

I did not bother to RSVP, as the party was immediate. - Now!
I smiled and went into my secret place - my room.
The party would begin with my 'just desserts!'

"OH LORD! MAKE THEM PAY -
THAT PERSON WHO HURT ME!
Make them pay!"

I GOT LOUDER.

"Make them suffer equally!
Every pain on me: to be
ON THEM TEN-FOLD!

Lord hear my prayer!
I know you don't like me to suffer.
I am innocent!
I did no wrong let them pay!"

I blubbed even more and my make-up ran.
My dress got crushed and spoiled,
my hair in disarray - unkempt.
My party was only just beginning!

My RSVP was never going to be read because I would not,
could not respond.
The envelope fluttered to the ground.
On the back 'RETURN TO SENDER.'

In bold capitals was 'MY NAME!'
WELCOME TO THE PITY PARTY!

Plaster Saint

The plaster saint was priced and put in the window.
Many artefacts and treasures surround it, but it had centre stage!

The spotlight was on it, the velvet glowed beneath its feet.
Many passed the window, at the shrine; many gazed on its beauty.
Its hands were lifted in praise and blessed the onlookers.

The saint's eyes were painted, blue and gold - surround red lips.
The plaster saints garments had been carefully chiselled.
They had turned and swirled, to show the grace and form.
Small feet peeked from the simple gown, in golden sandals.

The plaster saint was copied again and again - until that day!
That day - when another saint was glorified!

This saint was taller, and stronger, and more beautiful.
This saint had a halo that gleamed even more brightly!

The first saint was relegated to a shelf in the shop.
Not quite at the back - because of it's past prominence.
The people did not gasp in awe anymore!
There were others to admire.

Don't be a plaster saint - don't copy what is not yours!
Your plaster will be gilded, yes! - But you are not real!

Stone is outside of you - but you are flesh and blood!
Don't be a 'plaster saint', be a flesh, a flash, a glory in skin.
Don't copy. Be real.
Be the centre of his heart, not fixed in stone!
Don't get relegated to the back when you could be in GLORY!

The Joke

What makes you laugh?
What makes you throw back your head and roar?
What lifts your heart and soul and tickles you?
It fills your lungs with living air -
the air that circles the world and makes life!

Your tummy aches because laughter cannot stop.
What makes you laugh?

The biggest joke has not been told yet.
The biggest laugh has not been heard yet!
No comedian has screwed up his face, and given the punch line.
Not yet! Not this year!

What is the biggest laugh, the loudest chuckle!
I'll tell you what the biggest laugh will be all about.

The laughter of joy - not of pain or ridicule!
The laughter that shakes the atoms of the universe!
They dance and collide and make a merry tune.
They make the babbling brook laugh beyond its bank.

The biggest laugh - has the largest face.
The grin goes from ear to ear, from east to west!
The biggest laugh has no tears, or spite behind it!

The 'Big Man' himself, throws back his head.
He LAUGHS and LAUGHS and LAUGHS!

AS ALL HIS CHILDREN COME HOME!

This Place

There's a gap here for you.
A space with your name on it.
A place that has your hands and mind imprinted on it.
A place set aside and yet part of the whole.
A place that has been dedicated by God for you!

This place can be lonely and sad.
It can be full of joy and hope.
It sees with your eyes and your mind.
It feels with your emotions and your imaginings.
It's the gap fashioned by God in his image.
It is lost without you.

It is made just for you - no other can fill.
It is not perfect, it has its faults.
It is under the hand of God.
Under his love and presence.
It has pierced the centre.
BE IN THIS PLACE!

Hooked

It's a struggle Lord.
Each day I try to follow you - but temptation gets in the way.

"Tell me child what is in the way?"

"I do not feel love for my spouse.
I hate my neighbours, I am cold.
I don't like this but what can I do?

IT'S A STRUGGLE LORD.
Each day I try to be perfect.
I don't swear, I don't drink, I am dry.
I don't like this but what can I do?

IT'S A STRUGGLE LORD.
Each day I gaze at other men - longingly.
My struggle is hidden, I hurt.
I don't like this but what can I do.

IT'S A STRUGGLE LORD.
Others know about my spouse, my neighbours,
my coldness.
Others know about my perfection, my clean mouth,
my abstinence."

"Go on my child."

My face fell. How could I tell him of my worst guilt?

"Go on my child, I am listening, I am bending to hear."

"I am a man and love men as I should not.
I am the unspeakable."

"My child, my dearest child!
Have you not approached me because of your sin.
Have you not asked me - many times -
to help in your struggle!

I released my Son to die for all your sin!
you will still struggle!

But I AM WITH YOU because you know all your sin -
and seek my face!"

Curiosity

I have come here out of curiosity, but indifference is in my heart.
I don't want to know you!

I sit and hear your words strange to me like 'unconditional love.'
No-one can love like that!

I turn my heart to the wall while around me there is singing.
I don't want to hear you!

I harden my mind to stop the message from getting in.
I don't want to change!

I see the smiling eyes and laughing faces on others.
I have lost the will to dance inside.
AM I LOST?

The words start to pound in my heart, can I live again?
I would like to know?

I hear music that comes from outside my soul.
I would like to feel this love!

My heart wants to melt, but I am totally unworthy.
I want these truths to cover me.

I tried to escape from you, but my soul has been captured.
I am changed by your grace.

I have accepted you and I'm recreated by the 'Eternal'.
I am home - I am now in the light.

I AM SAVED!

20

Top Dog

"How can I reach the standard - reach the target?
How can I stretch beyond my height and soar?
How can I be above all others - in a space of my own?
How can I topple giants - win hearts - be the victor?"

My soul is the top of the league - the place of nobility.
My birth was poor I heard the secret - so off I go.
I read the book, got the right hair cut, smiled a lot.

My appointments were many, my shoulders slapped and praised.
I have got there, I have succeeded, what a joy!

ALL THE WORLD IS MINE!
No longer am I the minority, the worm!
My picture is in all the media - my words are examined.
My feet are shod in handmade and designer is my badge.
I was in the centre - lifted up - EXALTED!

It went even more than that!
My head felt light and joyous.

I looked down on everyone -
what a long way away they were!

How small they looked - how puny -
how lower class!

I shined my links on my sleeve, my face in the golden light.
I dripped respectability; my head was above my parapet!

I could not be caught or rivalled or bettered.
I am a self-made man!
The one to look up to!

What else could I be but the best!
IT WAS MY DESTINY!

BANG!... went the lid.
"Oh dear! What was that?"

"Oh foolish one, you are DEAD!" said the man next to me.

"The fastest way DOWN is UP. And you are ON TOP!"

Weep in the Dark Place

To weep no more is my aim.
Whose hands are steady enough for me?
Whose feet are the ones to guide me?
It is the Lord's!

The Lord sees in the dark place.
The Lord's voice calls out in the silence -
but is not lost there.

His ears listen to every whisper and sigh.
His arms reach out in the darkness to hold me.
He is not of the darkness, light is his home.

His hands that held carpenters tools are now gentle.
His feet that walked the dust of the earth - have stood on jasper.
His voice raised the dead also made the oceans roar.

What a Saviour is this!
What a Redeemer!

The Beginning and the Ending are His.
His Glory is given over to the Eternal Father.

They are One and I AM HOME!

Plastic Surgery

Why did I buy this, it was so good, it was mine?
Why did I get so excited?

It was the latest the best it was new!
Why did I not use it but stroke the box and hide it away?

It's been gathering dust, secretly.
It's been out of sight, out of mind.

My credit card proves I bought it!
Or did it buy me?
It was SO GOOD!

But it is now dust.
I don't get excited any more.

The newest, shiniest, best object I must have.
The old is disregarded and forgotten.
The newest is not used, I meant to?
Didn't I?

The adverts had blazed out at me!
The secret whispers in the darkened room -
with a window of light in the corner.

What a travesty, what a waste!

I kid myself the profit from my purchase helped someone -
but what if we all stopped and bought only what we need?

What if we used all that we have?
Will it all go around?
Will there be enough for the poor?

O foolish person, what am I talking about?
Is it just money, possessions, status.

NO ITS LIFE ITSELF!

What am I wasting?

WHO WILL PURCHASE ME?

Get Warmed

How do I get close to you?
Do I get close like warming against a fire?
Do I put warm covers over me to protect and hide!

How do I do this thing that is so difficult?
Why does it elude me when I most need it?
When I most need you?
When my power is gone and my legs weak!

The time speeds by and I am lost.
I AM NOT CLOSE.

The time appears to wander like a cloud and is gone.

Sharp words to myself don't help,
they are drowned by - my pain and anger and defeat!

How do I get close was the question - I ask again and again?

The answer is staring me in the face!

The answer has a hill to climb and mouths to feed.
The answer has dust on his face and scars on his back!
The answer is the answer he has always been.

I DON'T GET CLOSE TO HIM BECAUSE HE IS CLOSE ALREADY!

In a Box

"Don't call me paranoid, I just don't trust you!
Don't call me fearful, I just don't like you!
Don't call me selfish, I just don't want nearness!

It's been banged into my head by helpful people -
those that smile and say its OK.
TRUST ME.

Trust went out years ago with my innocence.

"Don't call me foolish,
I know what I am doing!
Don't call me isolated,
I know my own company!
I've got my life sorted out, my way, my boundaries are set.
My way is planned,
I trust me!

Don't categorize me, don't put me in a box!
I'm more complicated.
I'm more deep, than you think, than you ever know!

Don't you see, don't you understand?
I know I'm in a corner in my mind.
I know I would like to break out - and be free like others around.

I know I'm me - but me is not alive.
I have not changed.

Part of me cries out 'help'.
Most of me says 'Not on your nelly.'
Part of me is blanked off - kept secret even from myself.

OOPS - my eyes have met yours.
I DID NOT WANT THAT!
You only wanted to say 'Hello'.

I ONLY WANTED DEATH!
The life I really need, want and love is for the taking.

BUT I'M IN THIS HELL HOLE –

HELP ME!"

The Visitor

There's a mouse in my kitchen - it scuttles near the wall.
It runs and hides as lights go on - its soil left as a clue.
I did not know it resided here - or how long it will stay.
It's whispering nose and glossy eyes -
are not this cats prey!

I stalk the mouse at dead of night. I bung up its retreat.
But this mouse is small and crafty - its feet a gentle beat.

It eats the crumbs I've left behind, growing fat on my debris.
I clean and sweep and wash and beat and cover every breeze.

The rat-man costs too much to call.
I daren't give up I say.
Perhaps this mouse will find a fatter home -
and quickly go away!

I should have spotted it before but secret are his ways.
It sneaks in unawares, you know - before you - spot his tail!

I thought about my life today - that carries on this way.
The thoughts and feelings hiding there -
that should now go away!
These sins and sores and knowing pains -
disease and hidden care.
These should be trapped - and killed -
and also be laid bare.

I do not know when my visitor small will go -
away from me!
I only know to call the One that exterminates - you see!

The One who can trap - it by the tail -
and never let it go!
He's greater than the thing today - that crawls in the below.

I open parts of me to dust and clean and polish.
But don't look now! He's got the plan.
To clean out and to demolish!
To check each day and keep abreast the truth of living cleanly.
To bow each time a sin appears.

REPENT for it's his booty!

Propagation

What makes your leaves grow?
What makes you stretch tall and joys your heart?
What courses through you that is not obvious to the neighbours?
The ones who only see the straight upright person you present.

It seems a small interest as small as a mustard seed.
It seems insignificant even to you, you have not nurtured it.

The leaf buds are always there waiting for the warmth.
The warmth of your heart beating with excitement.

It's the one thing that makes you tick the special thing, unique!
What makes your leaves grow your buds shoot?

Your branches in your mind join and bring the rush like spring.
Your roots had been cramped by the rubble many years ago.

Best not to disturb it; it will cause you pain to stand free!
What if you decide to stretch - to move a different way?

The wind blows from the north and the east - don't get stuck!

Reach out but also reach down!
You don't sow on your own.
Draw in the blood life that is for you and you alone.
The blood life that has coursed through you for many years.

The Holy Spirit of God. 'You' - the interest!

Stretch out reach down draw-up the life!

The heartfelt breath - the uniqueness that is you.

You alone can be you; blossom, fruit, flourish in your uniqueness.
Don't get cut off – GET GRAFTED IN!

Do it Now

If left alone things gather dust, they get hidden.
The year turns to another year and things are forgotten.

Visitors try to pay no-attention to your life.
They turn a blind eye and say 'We cannot help.'

When they leave they say 'Don't go there again.

Cross him off our list.
They are trouble!'

The dust appears the same it cannot get higher.
Your eyes are so used to it you don't notice.
You pick your way around the stacks of papers and rubbish.
Detritus is everywhere, but you only see ahead of yourself.

Even when others say: '
We will help you clear up!
Put your house in order.
Shape up, be clean!'
Even that has no meaning to a soul in darkness.

How can darkness understand the light?
How can a person so low, reach up?
How can space be found to breathe?
Even curtains cover the eyes, and the soul hides?

A breath of God is felt in a breeze -
through a crack under the door.

Someone is cleaning outside and dust is -
scattered by a broom.

Water is splashed over the cobbles and -
innocent games are remembered.

It is spring cleaning time - the time of refreshing.

YOU ARE ALIVE!

Today

Tomorrow - can be too big for us.
It's difficult to live through today.
It gets dark outside; the wind blows the -
trees till they bend.

Tomorrow can bring fear to us - but we -
don't see the joy to come.
Our eyes close in sleep fearing tomorrow.

But tomorrow and today can be –
of great blessing and great peace.
It dwells close to all of us in the eyes -
of our loved ones and the voices of our children.

It dwells in the words of songs and colours of the rainbow.
It is beside us, beneath us, around us and through us.
That peace is love.
Love comes from the One who is Love.
That love brings power to us when we are weak!

Praise God for his love for each of us personally.
Praise God for 'Life Eternal' that awaits all who trust in him.

Tomorrow has this love and peace; we can't escape this!
Draw strength every second - every hour and every day.

MAY HIS PEACE BE WITH YOU ALWAYS AND FOREVER!

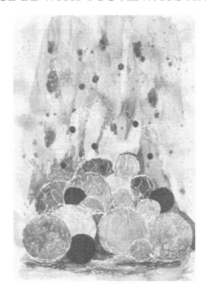

Take Eat

Freshly baked each day, the smell rises and opens our appetites.
The thought of old now made new.
It's impossible!

Hunger can be lost - through sickness and neglect.
Hearts just get colder and older - but can they become wiser?

Old sayings come from previous generations, they have learned.
DO WE LISTEN TO THEM?

The smell rises up the next morning - and we still find it difficult to eat.
Too much of a hurry, we'll snatch something later.
The appetite sets smaller and we starve –
in a kitchen full of good things.

How do we get appetite back?
The sickness has taken us over!

We don't eat a heavy meal.
We get tempted by little dishes arranged in a pleasing manner.
We take a spoonful, and find it difficult to taste - our mouths are so dry.
We take another spoonful, that's better that tastes good.
I want some more!

The next morning we are seated early and dreaming of -
fresh bread and wanting it to hurry up.

We all get stale we all get crusty, why was it neglected, by illness of sin.

Why not spread butter on it, eat, enjoy, hand it around.

FOOD IS BEST SHARED.

The Partnership

The days pass one at a time, sometimes merging into a blur.
Joys and pain get mingled on the same day.
We dance from foot to foot to keep up.
The speed of life can pass us by, but can slow down suddenly -
when pain arrives.

The strength to live this way cannot come from just ourselves.
The hope and joy for each day is magnified when shared.

Trials and troubles are halved or become liveable -
when a friendly face is looking at you.

The greatest thing is to know in all things - we are not alone.
The greatest thing is to share in other lives also.
The foolish thing is to cut yourself off and live in a cocoon.
Freedom to fly!

The grand plan for the universe is partnership.
A sharing with the Father of us all.
He gives us others to share this life with us.
Our partners in the home, our partners at work -
in the streets, across the pews.

It's good to hold hands and to laugh, and love, and sorrow.
We get supported by each other and by the strongest arms of all!
Our 'Blessed' Lord and friend,
our partner, supporter, comforter -
joy-keeper and sharer.

What a mercy from God that we have Him!
What a joy that the Lord has his Father and his Spirit!

How can we ever feel alone with all these supporting us?
Only our imagination, fears and past hurts separate us -
from each other.
"Smile at your partner in the home -
in the streets and in the pews.
Smile also with and through, enjoy the Eternal Partner.

TOGETHER!"

Conflict

To hate is very easy, to love is very hard.
It was bottles at first, stones, bricks and vulgar words.
Bombs strapped to bodies of men and women too-young to die!
The last gasp - that kills others that have different faces.

The dust never settles, the memories bury deep.
The ruins of lives - only a glimpse on the box in the corner.
The time passes too slowly to grieve - too fast to stop!
To hate is easy!

The faces of anger and pain on both sides are the same.
The hands that cause death are the same.
Humanity stares in disbelief.

'WE CANNOT BE SO CRUEL?'

The place of the Saviour's birth is surrounded.
Starvation, dirt and obscenities fill the air.
Holy voices cry to the Father for his salvation.
What can we do, what can be done?

The Lord himself saw what harrowing sorrows we inflict.
He felt the pain of dead children, widow's mourning -
old men with no hope.
The young with fright in their eyes.
It is the centre of the earth!
He gazes on it.

HOLY FATHER MAKE IT THE PLACE OF PEACE AGAIN.
THE CITY ON THE HILL.

THE PLACE OF PILGRIMS.
THE WONDER OF YOUR LOVE SET IN STONES.

When You Pray

Dare I ask, for myself alone?
Dare I speak, only of things of you!
Can I control my selfish thoughts and think only of you?
The struggle is hard when I try.
Am I speaking about myself again?
The effort is too hard.
There I go again thinking about my needs.

"Holy Father it's difficult!" I cry.
Even that point's to myself!

The 'Way' is hard, you said.
The 'Way' is narrow, you said.

Too much truth in those words!
I must press on; I must reach the mark even that is of self.

THE TRUTH?

You know my weaknesses, my inward thoughts;
my struggles to give you glory;
my fight against myself.
My way is not your way.

But in your truth I am pointing in your direction.
In your truth only – am I acceptable to you.
In your truth only – am I heard even above my sin?
In your truth I am lovingly restored to gaze at you.
You know my frame!
KEEP ME IN YOUR 'WAY'.

Scapegoat

Sin has to go somewhere, it has no home.
Sin wanders the desert, no voice talks to him.
Sin finds no watering-hole, no place to find rest.
No place to hide from itself, no peace!

Sin feels dark alone - it knows of no company.
It has to be quiet.
Sin cannot feel solace in others - for they are out of reach.
It crouches in the sand waiting for the end -
but it does not come.
It cannot hide; all is revealed in the noon-day heat.

The darkness is so dark sin cannot feel anything -
see anything.
There are no stars to guide, no lights to shine.
Sin is alone.

He cannot be shared - he cannot change, he cannot hope!
He has no master to look at - no flame of pity follows him.

He stumbles and falls.
No-one picks him up.
His head hurts with sorrow.
The stones bruise him.

Sharp pain fills his soul; there is no pity for sin.
Sin is an outcast - but he is not alone!
Others suffer with him.
Others accuse him of his failure.

Sin has no face.
It is covered with death -
for death is his home.

The mocking face of the liar of time haunts him -
saying all is lost.

IT'S TOO LATE; IT'S TOO LATE!

The enemy grins.

He has won at the place called Calvary!

34

The Sentence Is!

How strong is grace? Does its bars hold me?
Do I feel safe, secure - even when my sentence is called?

My sentence was death before I was born.
Before I uttered my first cry - my first breath-gasped!

The judge had put a black cloth on his head.
Sentence was passed! I was condemned!

The cell was not what I expected.
The death - not darkness?

I had not been given the right cell, the right punishment.

There was clean water: a clean bed.
Fresh air to breathe!
I could not see the boundaries of the cell.
The compass was lost.
As I entered, green grass sprouted, shoots of spring on trees!

I could not believe this. It was a dream. - It was unreal.

I turned around in disgust of myself, hammering on the door.
"Let me out!"

"I don't belong here! I've done wrong!"

Did nobody hear what the judge said – 'By the neck until dead!'

The ink was not even dry on the book.
The seal was attached.
The man read it out to my mind.
You <u>were</u> 'sentenced to death.'
But this place has been set aside for you.
For eternity - <u>there is no escape</u>!

This place is 'GRACE!'
Its walls are the heart of GOD.
Its floor is a righteous life.
Its ceiling the sky of faith.
IT'S DOOR THE BLOOD OF THE LAMB.

You alone have the key to stay or go!
You can put it in your pocket and stay.
Or GO to your old life - and be a PRISONER!

Fashion Statement

"Why do you wear that around your neck, do you know?
It looks beautiful, shows of your neck - but WHY? WHY?
Is it a talisman, a good luck, symbol, a charm?"
It brings beauty in its precious stones.

You say it brings harmony and peace -
matched to your sign.
The cross glows and shines and glorifies you!
There is no real meaning - your heart knows -
in what you wear.

It's just a trinket - a fashion statement -
a sales ploy.
It's just a passing fad lost in the junk jewellery box.
It will soon pass by and another to replace it.
There are always next season's colours - styles to escape to!

Where have I heard this before?
My mind remembers - the 'old old story'

Just a passing fad - a short gasp in history.
That's what the priest said, didn't he?
If it's made by man it fails!
It fails to live up to expectations.
It fails to bring harmony and glory.
IT FAILS TO GLORIFY GOD!

I'm back to the beginning again!
Is it like a stone around your neck?
A bauble, a trifle, a Sunday show off -
or is it as it REALLY IS.

Is it a symbol, a reminder of a sacrifice?
The reminder of heaven breaching earth's heart!

The original was not made of precious jewels -
encrusted gold.
The original was not hand painted -
craftsmen's passion or icon.
The original colour was red of blood and -
rough hewn wood.
The original does not hang around a neck of flesh and fashion!
The original hangs in the heart of God.
THE TRUE PLACE, THE RIGHT PLACE, THE ONLY PLACE.

Silence in Court

"Who will pray for me?
Who will speak a gentle word on my behalf?
Who will even consider my case?
Who will even read my sins out loud?"

I asked again and again, I could not in words -
but in sighs!
I asked again and again -
but heads were turned aside.

"Who will pray for me, who will be my help - my succour?"

The case has piled up against me.
The charges read aloud.
The judge looks sternly at the jury and says -
"You may be dismissed!"

The jury file out to decide the verdict.

I'm already guilty, my heart tells me this.
Who will pray for me who will plead, who will speak up?

A figure comes to me. It is very close and surprises me.
I look over the rail and a face meets mine and says -
"Did you hear the 'Voice' calling you?"

The 'Voice' comes louder - "I will speak!"

I cannot trace the sound, I cannot see my saviour.
The 'Voice' is even louder

"I will speak! I have spoken, I will speak again!"
The 'Voice' then says -
"Fear not! I will always speak on your behalf.
I have always been here pleading your case, I have never been stilled!"

"Why did I not hear you, I cry?
Why did you not shout to give me hope?"

"I cannot shout. I cannot raise the roof.
I'm the 'still small voice' - the Holy One of God.
The One who remained silent for Himself -
but speaks for you always.

Your Advocate. I AM"

God's Child

The God I know - loves me as a father.
The God I know - weeps when I turn from him and is jealous.
The God I know - wants the best for me even if it hurts.
The God I know - ran towards me when I came home.

The God I know - is far stronger than any enemy of mine.
The God I know - is warm and soft to my soul. He whispers to me.
The God I know - walks up a mountain and shows me possibilities.

The God I know - does not flinch in telling me my sin.
The God I know - points to my soul and opens my eyes.
The God I know - is patient beyond belief,
gracious in his dealings with me.
Is just and will not let me die in my sin.

But the God I know - has given me the choice to follow.
The God I know - becomes too quiet to hear when I decide not to listen.
The God I know - forgives 'seventy-time's seven'.

What a God I have! What a God you have!
What delight - what joy - what hope do you experience?

If you experience only condemnation, ask him why?
If you experience his Presence, thank him!
God is out for you, he seeks you with a passion.
Praise his name - PRAISE YOUR HOLY GOD.

38

Look this Way

Would a miracle turn your head?
Would it make you 'believe?'
Would seeing it with your own eyes make it real?
Would straightened limbs - sight to eyes - mouth to speak.
Really change you and make you mine?

I could give you a miracle a head turning–turn.
A showman's tool used in the wrong way.
How long - would faith last?
How long would it make-believe?
How long - before belief waned and died?
How long - before manna from heaven was stopped?

You only believe in the belief of today.
You are shallow!
The child in you hopes the next day - you never know?
Today may see another miracle - another cure.
You hope that it can all be proven - be scientific - be real and solid.

You listened to the wise ones - the one's who have studied -
and know the rights and wrongs of the universe.
The one's who eventually believe in nothing!
Nothing of worth. - Nothing of value or eternal.

The hope of a child is still in you - still available!
The world is harsh and does not believe.
FAITH does not rely on cleverness it 'JUST IS!'
FAITH is the miracle that's free - GRAB IT!

Constancy

You said 'Your love was an everlasting love!'
You said that - 'You loved me before the world began!'

I look around the world and see pain, struggle and strife.
I see the look in the eyes of the sick and see their desolation.

What proof do I have of your love?
What sign do I have that your love exists?
What power holds this love together?

I look for your love.
Is it hiding? Has it gone away?
Does your passion die for thinking of my rebellion?
Does this love change and shift like the sea?
Does this love remain in one place?
But seek another to love and leave me cold.
Does this love I see remain, is it true and reliable?

YES IT IS TRUE! It is from before the world began!

It is not like the sea shifting -
then moves to another.
What proof, what sign do I have of your constancy?

The sign of the cross.
The place you show your love to me.
The cross. The eternal centre of your love.
There all pain and passion meet.
Your love is shown.
Your love endures.
Your love is eternal!

Your arms are open to me.
Your heart waits for me!
You wait to surround me with love.

HOW CAN I STAY AWAY?

Christmas Cheer

It's that time of year again.
A time of twinkling lights, merriment and good cheer.
It's the time of holly and cards and -
meeting loved ones.
Of breaking barriers of harsh realities of life.

It's a time of meeting and greeting of saying -
you will keep in touch.
The time of unlit candles that were left in the dark.

No matter how we feel;
we are supposed to feel joy.
No matter how we speak;
we are supposed to be kind.
It can be such a farce when you look -
inside yourself and it is empty!

You said you would send out plenty of cards this year.
You had a heart that aches to contact others -
but you feel unworthy.
You spent little on gifts not because you are poor -
but because you are broken:
No contact to the source.

The Christmas card you sent was the cheapest - because you feel cheap.
There is no gift to send because the cost is too high!
The holy gift has not been accepted by you.
The ribbon is still tied.

Open your heart to the giver of Life!
Open your soul to the giver of Christmas.
Do it now. It might be the LAST CHANCE!

Thought Police

The Bible was SHUT, the words now silenced.
The pulpits now empty, the pews in a lonely line.
The people had gone, had been scattered, had been shaken.
The word must not be spoken again - must not be voiced.
THERE MUST BE SILENCE!
Even thoughts were searched out.

"Tell us how you feel. Tell us who you worship?
Tell us that God does not exist, that we are the reality?

Your righteousness sickens us - makes us vomit!
Your praises to your dead God - are crumbling to dust.
You cannot fight us!
YOU WILL NOT WIN!

Raise your hands to the god of reality - of science - of wealth.
Raise your hands to self-worth - to self-healing - to self-sufficiency.
Raise your hands. Let go - be like us - be as one - be popular!
Be on the front of the magazines - be like up to date fashion.
Be the bees-knees, worship self-worship. All of yourself!"

"WE CAN'T FIGHT THESE!"
Said a voice from the back.
"They are too strong!
We can't destroy!
We can't overcome these people!
They are too many, we are too few!
We can't destroy all the pressures.
ALL THESE TEMPTATIONS!"

"YES, WE CAN!" A voice near the door cried!
"LOOK at the sunshine outside!
Do you control dark and light?
No! - Can I? - No! -
But someone else does!
SOMEONE HIGHER - LARGER AND WIDER THAN US!"

The only thing we can do is show the light.
Show the sunlight while it is day.
The shadows will grow pale.
In this - smallness wins - selflessness reigns.

REFLECT THIS GLORY!

Unnoticed

It was only a slip of paper thrown aside forgotten.
It had no more use left, a receipt, a bus ticket now void.
The piles of rubbish all made up from single–items.
The piles of debris made with many hands all innocent!
All saying it's only one-piece - it was unnoticed.

Nothing is unnoticed.
Nothing is overlooked, forgotten or void.
Nothing is cast aside.

It's not time for collection yet.

The dawn comes up - the bins are being emptied.
The clatter down the street warns us it's coming - be quick!

The smell of spilt and tattered remains wafts over the street.

They were all useful once - all new and now corrupted.

The men wend their way up the street.
A discarded dolls body -
displayed on the front of the vehicle.
The body of plastic was once cuddled by a child - and kissed!
Now it stares one eyed as it leads the way.

The bins are thrown up in the air and rubbish is squashed.
The men practiced in the art of removal weave their way.
They call on each house and each alley in turn.

It's not a pleasant job - but it's got to be done!
It's got to be finished!
Then next week around again!

The shutter is pulled down - the hand bangs on the cabin.

"ALL RIGHT MATE! DRIVE ON!"

The bins are empty -
waiting for next week's rubbish.

Broken Reed

The water is bitter at Mara.
It was supposed to be clear, sweet and good.
My soul was troubled and hurt.
I had expected to be quenched and healed!

The 'Word' had said 'No sickness would come!'
Or that is what I believed - what I felt!
My hand had scooped up the water;
I had no choice no-other spring.

My pains and hurts felt worse - not better!
I did not want to drink this water!
I did not wish to feel this thirst!

I lowered my hand into it again. A voice cried.
"You can be purified - be clean!
The water need not be clear.

The time of thirsting is always upon you.
You can live with this condition.
You can grow and survive!

The streams are healed in your soul by the blood of Christ!
You may feel sick - lost - gone, but you are at the source.
THE SOURCE OF ALL RIGHTEOUSNESS!"

Short Span

I saw a butterfly. It twisted - darted full of life and free.
It was a blue flash amongst the dust, dirt and noise.
It was amidst the commuters - hurry by - unseen unnoticed.
It was here among the throng and bustle.

It did not see it coming!
It could not hear the roar the rumble.
The train came from nowhere - with no thought of small stops.
The train made the ground shake and the air whirl.
The butterfly spun and dived - circled then died.
Its body unseen on the rails.

I saw another butterfly.
Its hopeful path misdirected.
Its busy warm joyful presence - also unnoticed!
It danced in amongst the queue in the wrong place.
It should be outside in the sun - searching for nectar.
I did not see how it ended.

There was another butterfly.
I did not see - or pointed out.

Its wings were a baby's hand reaching to the sky.
Its colour was a pale as sand and gold as honey.
Its life was short - a collector's trophy.
Its wings were pinioned - its flight cut short.
Its sorrows written on the edges of its folds.

It had changed once - from form to frame.
Could it be resurrected again - at this time.
Could it beat the system that holds us all?
That also holds us down!

HE DOES AND HE SOARS!

I Was There

The torn remnant says 'I was there.'
I moved into the cave where you slept, I was there.
I could have struck you down, murdered - killed in your bed!
I WAS THERE!'

You did not notice until someone pointed it out to you.
You did not see the gaping hole proving my visit.
What a shame - it's too late!

You were furious that no-one had spotted me or heard me.
You raised your weapons against me searching for me.
Your blood ran hot and cold with hate towards me.

I had done nothing to earn this hatred!
I had only served you.

Voices that had called out your name in admiration -
had called my name.
Hands raised in praise to you -
had grasped my arms aloft.

You were jealous - you had murder on your mind!

I showed you the cloth and said "I could have killed you."
You wanted to believe all I said about my love for you -
but you turned to your own nature and hated me.

The cloth fell from my hands and fingers - fallen to the dust.
I had shown you all I was and endangered my life for you.
I sacrificed my safety for you not living in exile in comfort.
I had come so close and yet you still shut me out!

LET ME IN. I LOVE YOU AND I SERVE YOU!

Longing Heart

Through the passion of love you were born and created.
Through the giving of self to another you were made whole.
The golden gift of life was poured out and you shone.
The life was created before you were perceived.

How small you are.
How tiny - how helpless!
But darkness covered the earth in sin and you were torn from me.

Not an easy birth, but cast out in shame.

I reached out to you even though justice was in charge!
I called to you through the centuries - but you would not come.
My heart longed for you. You had been taken from me!

I was angry at the darkness of sin, I couldn't even look.
My arms ached; they were outstretched for you!
The answer came to me!

My death and destruction would give life -
would bring you back!

My falling into the pit was the only answer -
you were far away.

My breast called out to hold you and bring you to myself.
My arms encircled you as a mother.

BUT YOU WOULD NOT COME.

"Did I die in vain; did I sacrifice myself for a lie?
My love was born out of passion for your redemption!
My soul aches for you - not just for a second, but eternity!

Do not pull away from me - **I LOVE YOU!**"

Broken Dreams

Christmas day is not the same without you.
Christmas cards above the mantle shine there still.
The man on the radio says Santa is coming, a thrill!

Listen if you dare - he is here!

Presents line the floor; choice foods galore.
Happy faces around the Christmas tree.

It is not the same without you.

Christmas drunks stagger up the road.
Singing songs out in the cold.
It's not the same as when I believed.

Mistletoe, tinsel and the fir tree.
It's empty of the message.
It's empty in the heart of me.
It's empty because Christmas has passed -
with no-one remembering the old old story!

A candle flickers in the dark guiding the carol choir.
What do they sing, what do they bring news about?

The best thing about Christmas is a new start -
a new heart, a new life!
The best thing about Christmas is the opening of God's heart!
The opening of the best surprise yet!

Christmas can be the same but only with you!

MERRY CHRISTMAS!

Mellow Meadow

Step into the meadow -
it is quiet and peaceful there.
The noise of the world has gone, the son shines on you

Your thoughts and emotions are stilled by the hum of glory.
Your mind is refreshed by the breeze of his Presence.
Drink at his stream of living water - that was tinted with his blood!

The rocks and pebbles glisten -
like the good blessings ready for you always.

You sit down and sigh and the grass envelops you.
Close your eyes and dream and ponder -
let yourself go - in him.
See his face is your mind; and hear his voice in your heart.
Feel his goodness surround you like a cloak.

This place is always waiting for you.
It never moves or goes away.
This place is not hard to find.
It needs no map or compass to show the way.
This place is always in his heart as he puts -
His arms around you and lets you rest.

Be at peace in this place.
You are always welcome.
You are always looked for.
You are always expected.

This place is always open to you.
This place is the centre of God's soul and love.
The place of sacrifice by his son.
The place of joy and glory of the Holy Spirit.

BE THERE!

Balancing Act

The wire was stretched across the chasm.
The crowd was all abuzz - with the excitement - will he fall?
The cameras were turning, necks were straining.
A gasp went out!

He had stood up on the wire his hands holding the balancing pole.

He shuffled forward one step at a time.
The crowd gasped and gawped as he wobbled.
Would he meet his death?

The excitement never waned, some fainted, some giggled nervously.
The bandsmen found it hard to play.

Silence overcame them all.

The halfway mark was reached and passed!
The tricks performed with gusto, but now the climb began.
The other side beckoned it was only a breath away.

The little girls hid behind their mothers skirts.
The boys were willing him to crash or survive!

Everyone was watching.

Would he make a false move at the last moment!

The crowd had excitement and anticipation in their throats.
They could not cry out - even if they wanted to.

The last stride - the last step.

It was accomplished!

He had got to the other side.
The pole outstretched had guided him!
The line he followed showed him 'The Way.'
He reached the other side, his face glowed.

HE HAD WON!

God's Child

What is the man like - who turns from your love and salvation?
What is the man like - that chooses his way?
The man whose heart has never been open -
to the truth of your love.

His eyes and ears are stopped by scales -
and he does not want them removed.

He lives the way he must and the way he likes.
He does not think of his immortal soul -
and the end of his existence.
He feels his existence will be lost -
if he places himself in you!
That man's treasure is himself! His own glory -
which soon dies.

What is the man like who turns to your love and salvation?
He is the man who has turned to 'The Way.'
His heart has been exposed to the truth - about himself -
and your loves solution.

His eyes and ears have been opened - not by his own hands -
but by your blessed hands.

He lives 'The Way' as best he can with honour to you -
even when his life is not his own.

He knows of no other than yourself -
and because of your love he will have life eternal.

He loses himself in you and because of this finds himself again!

The man is now a treasure in your hand.
AND WILL BECOME YOUR GLORY!

51

The Journey

The first step nearer to you was the hardest.
The second and third follow close behind.
Obedience spurs me on but my goal is love.
Pour out your love on me, take my hand.

The joy of your father is in your face.
The serenity of your heart is all around.

Let me surrender to your will and obey you!
Let my heart show its praise in worshipping you!
Let my soul leap for joy when you are near.

You never turn aside even when silence is all around.
You never lift your hand in undeserved punishment.
Your heart's desire is always to restore.

Take my hand and heart in yours.
This is the time that lasts for eternity!

What do you have in store for me?
I cannot imagine.
What purposes you have for me -
are beyond my comprehension.
What foes I will meet and what guardian angels to greet me?
I have not enough imaginings!

These and many more things you have in store for me.

My life is in your hands, won by your blood.
Let the first step be always ahead of me so each day brings -
a new challenge and closeness to you!

Let this be my everlasting story and journey with you!
MY LORD AND MY GOD!

Do Not

Do not be cast down - you have not fallen to the end of hope.
Do not be cast down - the fountain of life has been opened.
Do not be cast down - your face will be washed in joy.
Do not be cast down - your clothes will not be rags of sin.
Do not be cast down - your heart will again be warmed by light.
Do not be cast down!
Do not stay there!
Do not dwell in darkness!
Do not be swallowed in death!
Do not be angered by the arrows of sin!

You shall be renewed!
You shall be as white as snow.
You shall run in the meadows filled with love.
You shall worship your creator with a clean heart!
You shall sing praises with a pure voice.

You shall lift your face to his sunshine and rejoice!
You shall come home to his arms.
You shall rest on his shoulder.
You shall sleep in his breast.
YOU SHALL BE WITH GOD!

Restoration

The sacrifice is made.
The price is paid for sin.
The healing has now come to the nations.
The glory and grace of God is now for all creation.
The creation groans for the completion -
of the restoration work of God.

The 'Holy One' of Israel is to be lifted high -
for all men to see and be healed!

The grace of God abounds to those -
who forsake their lives and follow him.
The fullness of his mercy rests on all those He loves.

Does he not love the whole world?
But the world does not hear his voice.
Goodness and mercy shall follow me -
all the days of my life.

My cup overflows!
His bounty and glorious nature has been -
seen in a broken body -
the body of his son.

The son honours his father.
The son is also honoured.
May his glory reign eternally in our hearts.
And may our lives show -
his great love and mercy!

His Home

The dwelling place of the Lord is in my heart.
The place that has sin - and righteousness as a part.
The dwelling in my soul is a joy to me. How can I forget it.
The righteousness is given to me as I lift my soul to him.
The joy of his closeness is deep in my soul.

The place he inhabits is a place prepared by him.
The place in my soul is rocky deep and wide.
There are dark-gulleys that go beneath the earth of my soul.
But the dwelling of the Lord ensures -
that his light will penetrate that darkness.

He is not shamed by my sin -
He chose to come and live within me.
His home is here!

I struggle with the dark and light in my soul.
Sometimes I ignore it.
Pretend one or other is not there!

But the Lord sees all - feels all - covers all - reveals all!
He is the centre of my soul;
my soul looks to him.
The Eternal.
The size of a point of light - if I make him so!
The Eternal.
The only meaning in my universe -
if I make him so!

But he is always the same no matter how I treat him.
He is always searching, healing, communicating, loving -
when I have turned off the light.
The joy of the Lord is in my soul.
The joy of the Lord is the Lord!
"REMEMBER MY SOUL!"

He is always above, us and beside us, and in us.
He always looks for us, always busy with salvation.
Wait for him, stay with him. Do not be afraid of your sin!
For he died for all your sin and he did it to dwell in us.
Praise the Lord for his Presence.
Praise the Lord for his patience.
Praise the Lord for his plan.
GOD IS WITH US, DWELLING IN US.
SAVING US TO THE END - AND MORE.

Listening One

The silent prayers, the unheard words are all noticed by you.
Every sigh, anguish and laugh of joy is near your hearing.
The moment a thought is in my mind, before my -
mouth has formed the words -
You are already listening!

The words unspoken by friends - are always acknowledged - by you.
The silent sighs of no understanding are interpreted in truth - by you -
because you know the true way to pray -
and the reason each prayer is uttered.

You bless the one who prays -
and the one receiving your answer.
They can also be the same person!

Your mind is alert to every prayer and every request.
You bless the one who opens their mouth to -
speak on other's behalf.
You acknowledge to the heavens that you hear and know -
and answer all prayers.

"Holy Father, continue through your grace and love -
to answer all our deepest sighs -
both for ourselves and others.

Put your words in our hearts so we speak your language.

THE LANGUAGE OF LOVE!"

Word Power

The written word is so powerful.
It turns neighbour from neighbour.
It turns nations upside down.

The written word does not have to be completely true.
Only a part needs the benefit of truth.
The rest is make-believe.

The rest is from the heart of the man writing.
The reader adds from his own heart.
Where is the truth now?

The written word is powerful like a two-edged sword.
It cuts to the bone and marrow of the soul - it reveals!

The written word can be shut in a book unopened -
unused, unread, unnoticed.
The word has no power except in remembrance.
The memory of bad-of-ill - becomes distorted in memory -
and becomes worse.

The good things fall below the lines.

Why do we remember only the bad -
not the wholesome?

Words from his 'Word' are like breath.
Like bread, like life itself.
It stands on the shelf real proud - a witness to the visitor -
but it gathers dust.

Lift it off the shelf everyday!
Pray to the One who speaks through its pages.

DO NOT be conformed to the world opinions and reasoning.
Read the 'good news,' life is not just of bread!

Read, learn be chastened, cheered, lifted, revived and saved -

BY THE LIVING 'WORD'.

Foundation

Totally dependent on you.
On the air I breathe. It comes from you.
On the fire in the sky, on the sea that roars.
On the wings that fly and glide and soar.
On the cooing of the dove, on the bear in its den.

All are dependent. All held in check and vigour.
All atoms intertwined throughout the ground and sea and sky.
All dependent - all reliant - in all.
All under your rule.
Under your yeah or nay.

All with an allotted span - a time of life.
All with a purpose - a plan - a secret task unfolding.
None are insignificant. None slip away.
None are unseen, downtrodden or forgotten by you.

No atoms are lost - but renewed by the spoken word.
By resurrection - reconstruction - renewal - redemption.
All explode and implode to the glory of your tone.
Your voice has commanded it - created it - comforted it.

Your voice never lies.
Never gives hells destruction to his children.

Who are his children? All the above - all below -
all with the chance to choose!

All dependent on his mercy - love - justice and sacrifice!
All dependent ones! All for you!

He Speaks

Your Word is a lamp to my feet.
The 'Word' is Jesus.
Your Word is my strength and shield.
The 'Word' is Jesus.
Your Word is grace and truth and love.
The 'Word' is Jesus.

He shows all your compassion, all your kindness -
all your joy, all your hope.
He shows us in his hands and feet.
Your sacrifice for us - he is Jesus.

The time of hearing is still with us.
Let Your 'Word' be heard.
The time of restoration is here now.
Let your work build.
The time of showing 'The Way' is for a short time.

Let the Word extend its span.
Your 'Word' was from the beginning and is until the end.
Your 'Word' is what holds the universe together.
Your 'Word' is there if we care to listen.

Open our ears and help us to hear the shepherd's voice.
Let those that are his - come to him to be saved.
Let those among the rocks - crying out in pain -
come down and be healed!

Let your Word resound around the world.

SO EVEN THE WORLD THAT DOES NOT KNOW YOU HEARS!

Dark and Light

"Let there be light - and there was light!"
This is your command and your will.
The light shines out of the darkness and obliterates it.

You are the light in my life -
shimmering and dancing through my soul.
The soul you created has many colours -
and shades like the rainbow.

The light you shed on me and through me -
shows me up and shows my many faces.
The light you shed on me has come from your -
'Blessed Son' - and his sacrifice.
He said he had come to give life - and life in abundance!

I see and feel the many colours of myself -
the dark places and the light.
The joyous places and places of desolation.
The hard and soft parts - that both have to yield -
to your glorious light.

How can they live with each other if they have no central part?
No joining that is not of themselves?
They cannot live in harmony like the rainbow - on their own!
Only your Son's light and sacrifice is the atonement -
that joins all these things together.

Your 'grace' has said that you will live with me -
when I ask you in:
Your 'grace' sheds its atoning light on to my many facets -
and sheds a united rainbow!

I must not fear the dark and light inside me -
for fear is not of your light.
Your light brings comfort - and peace - and joy and love.
Your Presence is to be sought at all times -
for you are with me at all times.

The divisions in my soul are made perfect in your love.
The dark and light are joined in joy with you.

Lord, let your light come, let me revel in the many changes -
and patterns that your light brings to me and be healed!
For I am many and YOU ARE ONE!

Always the Same

The Lord of heaven, the changeless one, smiles on me.

His eyes are always showing love to his people.
He always stops to bless - He always looks for his servants.
His breath is always bathing our hearts with his grace and goodness.
He does not change or turn away

He has no side, no other faces to show us.
Parts of him are not hidden.

He is the Eternal, the Father of all, the Son of his people.
The Holy Spirit that gives grace, love and healing.
He does not change.
He speaks from the depths of the universe.
His anointing voice is always speaking.

He does not change.
Hold him if you can!
Grasp hold of this fact!
The Lord never changes, is steadfast and true.

THE LORD IS HIS NAME.

All Chosen

He could not bear to see them suffer.
He could not bear to see them fall.
The glory of his Presence was shattered - at the call of -
His flock - of his - people - of his beloved.

They had been chosen by him to be his people.
They had been raised up again and again -
but they would not heed him.
They would not heed him - they would not hold fast to him.

He turned aside and left them to evil times.
He shaded his face from them, but broke in pain for them!

They did not trust him.
Did not want him.
Did not believe him.
His truths and Presence were of no importance to them.

Time and again he sent his deliverers to bring them peace.
Time and again they despised his ways.

Why does he turn back after all these denials?
Why does he run his fingers over their hearts and cries for them?

Because he loves them as a father.
He loves them as their Saviour.
He cannot deny himself.
But he cannot leave them.

They turn to him - falsely - and he still forgives them.
What a sorrow they cause him!
He has to deal justly with them -
there is always a time of punishment.

Will they turn and repent; will they cleave to only him?
Only God knows the truth of their hearts.

BUT HE LOVES THEM!

Prove It

The people said "Prove it prove it so we can believe.
Prove it beyond a shadow of a doubt a scientific certainty.
The lies that people tell us how we can believe you!
They shout they scream they turn to a new piper
PROVE IT. PROVE IT. PROVE IT!"

"OK!" Said God "I'll prove it!
Who spoke with you and walked by your side in the garden?
Who never let you go in Babylon?
I moved the harp-strings.
I never forgot the lost sheep!
I never killed the scapegoat."

"THE PROOF IS STILL NOT ENOUGH!" WAS THE SHOUT.
"THE PROOF IS NOT ENOUGH TO SATISFY US!"

"I was with Joseph who was tempted to sin and didn't.
I was with David who fell, sinned and forgot himself.
I did not condemn but reached out to bring peace!"

"STILL NOT ENOUGH PROOF?
We follow all you told us in the past.
We split the herb to the tenth and hundredth -
that is our proof!

What can You do that is different to our way?
We have followed it from the beginning, we are satisfied!

I DON'T THINK WE EVEN WANT ANY PROOF ANYMORE!"

A large sigh was heard.

It thundered off the outer universe
It shook the atom.

"I have given the best proof - MYSELF!"

The Misunderstanding

It stung my heart - that you do not understand me.
It caused my mind to weep in turmoil for you.
My feelings are put aside as I pray for you.

The leper the crooked the lame the blind come willingly.
What do they see that you don't understand?
What makes them come up out of the crowd to be noticed?

It stung my heart - that you did not understand me.
I had spoken to you about love, mercy -
truth - but all you see is threat.

I do speak even now - even on a wind-swept hillside.
The leper the crooked the lame in spirit open their ears.
They hear they understand - there is no darkness!

You cower in the folds of your cloak –
plotting plans to kill.
Not intending to destroy me –
but to separate yourself from me.
Your heart you say is fine; it is in isolation, it stands up.
It goes its own way,
does its own thing,
does not join in.

It stung my heart - that you do not understand me.
My disciples give out bread and little fishes.
Food for you.
You are not hungry for the words I speak –
but you grab the food!
It's amazing the food slips down to your centre.
But not my words.

I have prayed for you - but there are others more willing to feed.
More receptive to my words and my motives.

But all you feel is the crumbs.

ALL YOU SEE IS MY BACK!

<u>Axis</u>

Did your father hear the cry as you were enveloped in sin?

Did he reach out to you - as you descended into hell!

Were his angels straining to hear your last breath?
Did the darkest hour be your most blessed time?

Your heart had stopped and you were gone -
to the place destined for us!

Your father mourned you - and the curtain was torn in two.
Great clouds of darkness covered the earth -
and the ground shook in pain.

THE ETERNAL HAD DIED!

M.M.

Just a minute is an aeon to me.

Just a second is like a thousand years.
Numbers that can be cold too - and inconceivable!

I am not a number I AM!

I AM with you.
Every part of your life is seen - felt,
experienced in clarity by me.

How can I - be distant because my hands are not solid.
How can I - be distant because of my nature.

Because I created all that you see - hear and understand -
they are not the truth about me -
but are part that you can understand.

I behold everything from your start in time - to the ending of time.
Do you think I don't belong in your life because of this.
Because I am unfathomable.

Think of the second my Son was born -
into your world and try to think of me -
not caring for you!
The part of me in you - is from my Son!
His Spirit lives in you -
NOW!

I AM not distant not too long, not too great -
to be out of your life.

But I AM around you, in you, before you -
behind you, above and below you.

FOREVER!

At Any Price?

The pearl in my hand had blood on it.
It could have stayed at the place if its birth -
enclosed in the shell, in darkness in secret.

The pearl I had sought was found - was hidden -
not to be lost but to be redeemed, a thing of beauty.
The pearl in my mind had not been forgotten.

I asked the Father "How much shall I sell? To buy it."
My treasures were so great and so high -
but the pearl was not my possession yet!

I pleaded with the Father to pay the remaining cost -
to purchase the best we had created!

The Father owned everything, knew everything -
coveted everything.

He hung his head and said,
"Are you prepared to pay the cost?
The cost is very high for the thing you want is removed from me!"

"I will pay any cost! I will give all I have! All I AM!
I want this treasure this seed of humanity!"

"The price is your life!" The Father said.
"The price is your banishment!" The Father said.
"The price is all you are! All your glory! Everything!"

I did not hang my head - but kissed -
my Father's face and said.

"I will go to the end of the earth!
My blood is the cost of this treasure.

I WILL PAY IT IN FULL!"

68

Together

He created you –
but that was not enough for God.
He breathed life into you –
but that was not the end.
He saw you grow tall and straight and your first steps.
He heard your first words and felt your joy in sunshine.

He was as close as a mother –
but still not enough!
He was as close as the cuddles of your own father -
but it was still not enough.
Not enough for the biggest heart.
Not enough for the Eternal One.

How could he make himself small enough to be close?
As a mother or father?
How could he be small enough - to hear your first words?

It's impossible we all say it's not imaginable.
He is too big!
Too far away to notice - to care - to participate in my life.

He even heard the shouts of derision at his plan to be small -
to be a part and essence of his created children.

He did not turn to the left or right - but made himself small.

First as a tiny babe at his mother's breast.
Then as a child with wisdom above his years.
Then as a carpenter with strong hands that -
caressed and shaped wood.

Then as a bleeding Saviour who only wished -
to be close to his children!

And now how close is he?
He lives by his Spirit inside us!
He resides there.
He joins in with the household of your soul -
and suffers and rejoices with you.

JUST AS HE WANTED TO!

Greatest Make-Over

The Father said "Why do you want to save them?
Why do you go after them when they despise you?
We created everything about them - from their cells to their souls.
We gave them life and form and being.
Why do you want to save those who are criminals?"

The Son gazed back at the Father in love and hope.
He said "Father I know that deep in your heart -
YOU WANT TO SAVE THEM! -
You want them to return!

I know they cannot look at you - unless they die.
They cannot hear your voice -
because of the distance between.

I know that many servants you have sent to -
lift them up - were killed by them.
They are witnesses here!

Their blood must not be spent needlessly they are a sacrifice.

Even the smallest lamb at Passover was -
a witness to your compassion.
The smallest, poorest of souls was -
able to partake with his neighbour.

At that time none were left out -
not even aliens and servants.

You tried to close the gap Father -
with the blood of the lambs.
You showed the possibility of redemption for all!

I want to save them for your sake! - Father. Not my own.

I have seen the love you have for them:
I AM WILLING TO GO!
To be the 'First Born' - the 'Living Sacrifice.'
The only One to fill the gap.

Father are we not ONE! -
Let my glory come back to you!
Let me do this greatest - small thing -

FOR THE ALMIGHTY LORD - MY FATHER!"

How Much! Father?

From darkest darkness I call.
I cannot slip any lower - any farther and still exist.

The darkness has no comfort, no pity, no love, no hope.

I SLIP AGAIN.

My throat is parched from calling to you, I cannot forget you.

I SLIP AGAIN.

Sin is a terrible darkness bringing pain of despair and loss.

I SLIP AGAIN.

My feet have lost their hold. My fingers torn and bleeding.

I SLIP AGAIN.

I have gone so far -
there is no more depth to go.
There is no lower place, no more empty;
no more desolate place.

But I chose to be here. I chose to fall. I chose to die!
I chose to be lost from you.
I cannot even scramble to the surface.

Earth's clods hit me in the face. I am smothered.

BUT I CHOSE TO BE HERE!

I chose to love you so much I had to leave you!
I had to lose your face.
Even the memory of you has now gone!

The darkness is so dark I cannot even be myself.
I am now fully sin. I am now fully lost.

The Father cries out - but I don't hear even now.
But then the glory of resurrection surrounds me

I call out "FATHER!"

Time Waster

What second of the day does he not touch every heart?
What time span is allowed for him to stand aside?
DOES he take a rest from his labours because of hearts attitude?
DOES he look at his creation for a minute and turns from earth's souls?
DOES he sneak a break, a time-out a siesta, a folding of hands?

He is always on the move in every heart, every hue every system.
He is constantly working to be heard - to be seen - to be accepted.
He is always on the march towards triumph - of the saved soul!
He does not see sin - but his Son stands in the way beckoning.
Beckoning the soul to give up - and give in to his kingship - his majesty.

No matter how we paint the other - no matter our bias - or belief.
No matter how we bend his ways. His way is true and constant.
He does not tire in his work.

Every soul you meet, greet, pass by, is sought by him.
Every tribe, race, gender, style of life, social standing, is fully open.
They may not believe, feel, see, his Presence.
They may not have merit in your eyes - but are of great value to him!

What a great treasure is around us - what a prize worth fighting for!
Not one missed out, not one unredeemable!
All are prizes to be claimed. His Spirit is on constant duty.
Praise God! That no one is left out or alone.
FOR HE IS THE CONSTANT ONE.

Smooth Sailing

Where will faith lead you, are you prepared?
Are you prepared for the unexpected - even failure!
You followed all the messages, confirmations and signs!
But has the way been blocked, dashed and corrupted.
You stand with your head in your hands weeping - to the sky.
"Why lead me so far?
Why shine as a light on my path that leads to - nothing!
Why have you done this?"
It went silent, silent as the grave.
You called again!
"Why do this? I heard your voice calling - I followed!"
SILENCE AGAIN.

You fell to your knees; you were embarrassed you were so sure.
You had heard. You had heard his call - so clearly!
You told everyone you knew.
You knew what God had in store for you - but still the silence.

The days grew longer and darker, the shutters fell.
Heaven had closed its mouth - it did not speak.
The grey light in your mind was out - it had died!
No spark left, no strength in your arms.
You reached the ground with a sickening sigh.

"No care from you!" You cried. "No word, no comfort!"
You were frustrated and angry, lost and alone.
Embers burnt your eyes to tears, your throat choked.
You fell in silence - the silence of helplessness.
There was a pause that seemed many years. You lost count.

The curtains would be drawn back by a finger, you would look.
You wanted to search the road. The path to follow.
Silence, silence, silence - a horrible dream.
You gave up trying!

You sank into the arms of the One - the only love of your soul.
Then you heard him again. It was beyond reckoning.
It was such a joy! - You never questioned him. - You dare not!
But he said "See I'm still here - I am always here!
You followed my voice till destruction came!
Now you are ready to do every task I have for you.
Follow me! No matter where I lead!"

You got up and stood with your guide!

Home Life

Jesus did a belly flop right into our lives!
He had grown up in a crowded house the oldest of children.
He had learned how to make wood mould under his hands.
He had splinter marks in his fingers and gouges on his palms.

Singing was heard from his mother and sisters as they cooked.
Water was brought from the well and water fights with his brothers.
His father had looked on with protecting eyes -
seeing that all is well with his family!

Times of work were plenty and tiring. Times of rest - few.
But he took the times of pleasure and lightness and brought joy.
Laughter rang through the house as a mouse -
was chased from the corn pots.
He helped his sisters carry water jars -
even though it was a girl's job!

He sang and clapped. In feasts - in trials.
Lifting his voice from treble, through to bass as he grew.
Not flinching from life's joys and pains when -
his father died.

His family mocked him!

His mother's tired face watched him -
from the corner.
As he piled up wood - that was to be prepared for a table or chair.

His mother grasped his face between her hands and kissed him.
He was ready for his second ministry.

His first was his home!
The second was the wide world so deep and cold.

HE PLUNGED RIGHT IN!

Woodwork

He was a carpenter used to the feel of wood.
He stroked the grain, inspected the warp and lie.
He chose and lifted. He held and pierced the wood -
bringing new life and shape to the lifeless block.

He worked away with his father, learning - leaning -
gleaning his father's knowledge: how to remake and renew.

He would stand up - satisfied that the work was good.
The work completed. The wood now used not abused.

He knew that wood could be warped and useless -
as he turned over the tables in the temple!
The wood splintered and cracked and became dangerous.
He cried to his Father - that they had not -
learned - the lesson that his house is holy.
A house of prayer.

He rested and waited for the result of his redirection -
restoration of faith and hope.

The answer was not short in coming.
It came like a fire!

The anger crackled around the wood - life extinguishing.
The fire of jealousy, power and hate licked upwards -
trying to consume the tinder-tender heart of the Saviour.
The Saviour who could change them and cut out their sin.
The Saviour who can make them straight and holy.
The Saviour on the tree of shame!
The Saviour held by nails…..

The Saviour opened and split for the sin of the world!

The Big Catch

The rope was thrown over the side again.
The net snaked out on the water and sank to the bottom.
There must be fish here, we are fishermen after all, and it's our job!

The net was pulled along and pulled out - hour after hour.
Tired men perspired even in the chilly air - the boat creaked underneath.
The wind should have picked up.
It was getting near morning.

For many years, many summers, toil and sweat for a pittance.
For many lonely nights, all for a small catch all for tax collectors!
The wind had dropped; the sun peeked over the hills.
Dawn had come - the nights fishing was drawing to a close.

The dreams of a large catch was disappearing in the mist.
Backs felt like they would break - throats were parched and dry.
The bottles of leather were held up - and water poured out.
It was good to drink, good to be refreshed, good to be alive!
They laughed and slapped each other on the back.
Tomorrow night would be better.
Would bring a huge harvest of fish!

The lone figure stood on the shore, and raised his hand to his eyes.
The glare of the sun was now brighter and getting hotter.

"Let me borrow your boat?" He called. "I have need of it."
The friends looked at each other, was this 'another catch?'
Something or someone with strange ideas!
You don't fish when the sun rises!

Ho-hum let's let the stranger into the boat.
You never know. He might be entertaining.
A small diversion on the way home.

But then he opened his mouth and spoke.
THEY WERE NEVER THE SAME

The Leader

I AM the 'Good Shepherd' of the sheep.
Each one is entrusted to me, and bound by my own blood - to me.
Each one's name is known by me and my heart hears their cries.

I move towards each one with my hand stretched out -
to feel every wound and every sorrow.
My voice is still and quiet - as I guide them through the desert.

The places of shelter and water are all known by me.
I will lead them all.
I am the 'GOOD SHEPHERD!'

Feel my side, and its wound that was made -
when I rescued you.

I love my sheep. I love my lambs.

LITTLE FLOCK – SPECIAL TO ME AND GREATLY LOVED!

Well, Well, Well

Will you give me a drink? He said.
Even to a stranger an enemy!

My thoughts are my problems my woes my estrangements.
My passions rule. My beliefs confuse me.
I have a searching heart!

I raised the water for you, puzzled!
My eyes see a man - who is supposed to hate.
Supposed not to speak to me. And even spit on me!

My mind tells me -
'why does this man <u>not</u> - treat me less than a dog?'

I look into his eyes and they are kind and questioning.
I ask him how come he is even speaking to me!
My heart flutters - unexpectedly. 'This is no ordinary man!'

The water sparkles in the ladle and in the cup.
He drinks it slowly.
He closes his eyes and offers the cup to me!
It's a free gift to an untouchable - an outcast!

"My gift to you is living water!
You won't have to run dry again!"

"Tell me where can I find the water you speak of, how far is it?
(What I meant was 'do I have to change before I drink')

He smiled a smile of great knowing and wisdom.
Told me about myself!

No secret was hidden.

My eyes were opened. My mouth was dry.
I wanted to drink - but others should know!

"They know about me.
Dare I tell them about him!
Dare I bring them to the 'Living Water!'

The One that was to come.
Is here!
and <u>will </u>return with LIFE ABUNDANT!"

Bountiful

The little fishes were a sign from you, of your Glory.
Your abundance that is given freely to men.
The time of forgiveness is now. The time of healing is now!

You give all of yourself freely to your people.
You give all of yourself to those that are lost - and far away.

Have pity and mercy on us all, Lord -
let your glory and compassion shine out and bring –
redemption to the world!

Let your loving kindness be seen by all.
Let the sound of your voice and -
command provide abundance.

And let grief be no more.

Let the lost rejoice in you.
Let the hungry be fed.
The Immortal Saviour has come to this world -
to show your love.

We can turn away or we can share your bounty with all.

Let this be so.
Let your work continue.
Let us bring your glorious harvest of love,
compassion, healing -
forgiveness, joy and peace to all men.

By your power only, by your love only.
For we are all sinners - saved by your Son's sacrifice.

Let all these blessings be known from the beginning-
unto the end forever and ever.

TO YOU BE THE GLORY, AMEN!

The Sleeper

He knew there was a storm coming - yet blue above the sky.
The resting place was in the boat - the men pulled ropes up high.
They lived their lives upon this sea - they knew of every time.
The incidents of sun and shade - of plenty and of prime.

The catches in the nets they bore - they counted and they paid.
But suddenly the sky was black - what called now was the grave!
They battled, weary arms reached high, they could not turn but drown.
The hail and wind and raging sea - would never be stepped round.

The sudden storm was tearing now - upon their troubled minds.
The wind whistled round the crew - and down the depths sublime.
They could not battle anymore - the peril was too keen.
Only an angel of God was there - to change the blighted scene!

The angel was soft of face - and slept within the bowels.
He dreamt a dream of many fish - and healing of the crowds.
"Wake up! Wake up!" The men called out. "We die - do you not care?
We have no strength to fight the storm - or enemy of the air."

"Be still! Be still." The angel said - the man they knew so well.
For Jesus had the Father's heart - and messages as well.
He stilled the storm in single word - the men 'gaped' open wide.
He said that they had not believed - for safety by his side.

They stood amazed their hearts stood still - for great was their dismay
They had trusted 'not' - the only one - controlling every day.
They laughed and clapped - and looked to God and amen's holy chord.
They never looked the same on Him.

The HOLY ONE Adored !

Living Life

When it was right, you walked away from the crowd.
When it was right, you slept in the throes of the storm.
When it was right, you moved to one side to the quiet place.

You did not hurry; you did not rush or use force.
You did not panic, that time was short, and much had to be done.
You did not watch the time pass, and raise your hands in sorrow.

You knew there was sufficient time for everything.
You knew what force to use for every task.

You were relaxed and worked with joy and patience.
You relaxed in the spaces that your Father arranged.
You did see the task ahead, but you always worked for the day.

You were never anxious over anything -
but still had compassion on your people.

When it is right - you work in our lives.
When it is right - you draw to one side.
When it is right - you suffer beside us.

Teach us how not to hurry.
How not to chase clouds.

Teach us how to rest our minds –
as well as our bodies and spirits.

Teach us your way of living -
AS WELL AS GIVING US LIFE!

Crunch Time

We were rowing the boat toward land -
tired and weary - from all the days work.

You were resting and watching our drawn faces and looking -
to the farthest shore.

We scrambled from the boat and walked up the bank -
our feet crunching on the pebbles.

You walked ahead of us - as usual.
A quiet expression on your face.

We turned the corner and what we saw,
made our hearts sink.
PEOPLE!

We saw your face turn from weariness to compassion.
Your hands beckoned everyone to sit down.
You spoke and taught many things to the hungry crowd.
They listened intently and drank in your words.

The sun had passed its peak and it grew darker.
It was time to leave!
We realised no one had eaten, no fires had been lit.
No movement had been seen all day.

The people were hungry and needed to be fed.
SOMEHOW?

What a predicament we did not even have -
enough money to buy food for ourselves!
Let alone a crowd.

Did you want us to spend what we had and more!
To feed them?
You asked "What did we have in the way of food?"
We showed you the loaves and fishes –
rather foolishly - thinking .
"What can be made of this trifle?"

You showed them and us - the abundance you give - in all things.
You showed us the love that you have - for all men!
You showed us all -
and EVERYONE WAS FED!

Triumphant Entry

You entered the city with praise in your ears.
"JESUS! JESUS!" your name was cried, save us, save us all!

You heard the praise and knew the heart of men -
how shallow it was.
How much trust you had, in those who yelled the loudest.
How much trust you had, in the smiles and knowing looks.
"JESUS! JESUS!" They cried. "Save us from the oppressor!"

You had to travel around in secret, the Passover had come.
Plans of men were made, a plot, a plan, money exchanged.
You remembered the cries and exaltations!

You only had a small band of followers, an elite.
Men who dreamt of victory during the day and spoke -
of the struggle during the night in quiet whispers.

You smiled in secret; they were all determined to follow you!
You knew that force would be used against you and them.
Do you escape through the back door - or step out into the light?

Your hand moved inside your cloak and felt the handle.
The handle of the knife that would be used to start the rebellion!
That would strike the soldier down.
The source of all the trouble!
"JESUS BAR ABBAS! JESUS BAR ABBAS!"
Was cried, was lifted high.

I was ready for my triumph, ready to die!
Ready to lead others to victory, ready for the revolution!

What a winner I would be!
Better than any pacifist, any friend of enemies.
Better than a collaborator.
Jesus the mover and shaker.

UNSTOPPABLE!

Servant-Hood

He did not have a sword - but a donkey.
He did not have a mighty army - but wore sandals.
He did not come in glory - but was the lowly carpenter.
He did not shout with the crowds - but whispered to children.
He did not raise his arms to strike the guilty - he wept for us!
He did not run from the opinion of man - but lived like his Father.

His joy, and peace, and hope, and energy -
light, and eagerness; tranquillity comes from doing -
things his Father's way.

He did not turn to the left or right.
He did not waiver or falter - but always looked for us!
He did not shy away from pain - but bore it for us.
He did not leave sin in our lives - but drank it for us.
He did all things as a sacrifice.
He obeyed his Father's heart -
He wept with joy - when he saw the outcome of his pain!

He looked at his sheep and did not abandon them.
Glory to him! - Glory to the Father! - Glory in his house!
Let his Spirit constantly reside in our hearts -
and let him continue his work.
Let him continue his 'Presence'.
For God Almighty and Holy, The beloved Son who died -
are all hidden in his Spirit!

Blessed be his ways.
Blessed be his hope.
Blessed be his peace.

BLESSED BE THE LORD ALMIGHTY!

What a Mistake

Our God was mistaken for a gardener -
by those who knew him, and loved him.
Our God got his hands calloused by working in wood.

His family jeered him and laughed behind his back.
Our God was looked at behind hands and his father maligned!
The neighbours loved to gossip, and put him down.

Then he was mistaken for a conqueror -
by the rabble who would chase after any messiah –
cheered him.
What mistaken identity - what a huge mishap!
The God of the universe - having a weakness - being a man!

Where are the golden chariots, the flames of fire?
The God we want - we expect!

Where is the flaming sword, the smoking ruins?
The God we want - we expect!

We've got it all wrong!

Our God was mistaken for a gardener.
His hands calloused by wood, were pinned to a wooden cross.

Our God was jeered at.

He was naked before them.

He was spat at by the people, who had praised him

I think we had a wrong idea about God!
He had the right idea about us!

WE NEEDED A GOD LIKE OURSELVES!

The Good Shepherd

Your rod has broken me.

You struck it hard - on my path and I cried in pain.
You smote my soul - with the pain of redemption.
I had kicked against you - and your love and plans for me.
I had baulked at your commandments and guidance.
I had eaten what I willed; I had drunk from the pit.

You looked on me in love but strained to hold your hand.
You knew that you could not let this continue.
You could not let me graze as I wished!

What a fool I'd been - what a selfish soul, what ignorance.
You raised your arm and struck me!
You struck me down from the high pit!

I tumbled down screaming in pain and shock.
You don't do this. You don't deliberately hurt!
My tears ran down my face stinging my skin.
My eyes were red with weeping. I hobbled!

I hobbled to you and cried out -
there was nowhere else to go!

I had already been there, but needed to be close to you.

I cried again and your strong arms picked me up - with care!
You did not want to inflict more pain - redemption had begun.

I rode on your shoulders, felt your warmth -
and slept by your heart beat!

I WAS WITH MY SHEPHERD.

Who's coming to dinner?

The table was set; all was ready, prepared, waiting.
The guests arrived, some chattering excited, some joking.
This night was always special, a time of remembrance.

One guest burst into song, a song of old, a song of triumph.
The others clapped and laughed and danced and joined in.
A happy crowd, a joyous group, a family of humanity.
They sang again, danced with joy and sang about Zion.

It was a special night, a night of togetherness and fellowship.
A night of harmony by voice and by the heart.

The little child asked the old, old question about the vacant chair.
The reply was given, heard many times by all who listened.
There will be a time of reconciliation, and restoration.

'Not this year? But let it be this year!'
They all thought.

They lifted high the platter that held the lamb and the bread.
They dipped and shared, and sometimes remembered old hurts.
They had been rescued from the shadow of death, so long ago.

It was getting late, the leader became quiet.
He spoke to the purse-holder and gazed into his eyes.
Face to face, breath to breath. They paused in eternity.
"Go and do what you will! - Be quick!" He said.

The friend left quickly, nobody was disturbed.

The feast was closing, the message was changed!
The leader broke the bread in two. His body declared!
The wine was poured and supped, drank to the depths.
"His body broken for you!" He cried, "His blood too!"
The men were startled, some tears in eyes.

"What will he be? A sacrifice?"

Imagine

Imagine the first taste of sin on the Saviour's lips!
Imagine the recoil at the sight - sound and fragrance of separation!
Imagine knowing at that instant the Father has fled from thee!
From thy Holy Presence.
All peace destroyed in an instant!

Imagine the screams to heaven.
The wrenching pain of degradation.
Imagine every sin - its foulness and stench filling you up.
Imagine every bone aching for release - oblivion but still-breath.

Still to breathe the unholy air - the sorrows of the world.

The stillness is a horror to you – distance – darkness - hell itself!

The boundary of sins grasp looms in your face - smothering-covering.
There is nowhere left - all sin explored - the chasm closed.
Darkness only darkness - no light - hope or joy remains.
The last sigh - swallowing the last of sin - ALL GONE!

Stillness reigns - for a second.

Then "GLORY - HE'S BACK!"

The Father gently touches his Son.
"It's done boy - completed!
Come home - back to glory - to your place!"

The Son lifted his head -
the crown of thorns - diadem spun.
The nails now hold him fast to redemptions plan.
He's won - he's overcome - he's got his children back!

Now time to die - time to leave for a short while.
He looks at his reward - his treasure - Adams man - blood bought.
His treasure - his joy - his kingdom in soil–made form.

"Into your hands!" He cries.

Heavens gates flung wide!
The invitation to all has been posted.

ALL is fulfilled.
AMEN!

Togetherness!

God the Father felt the nails that his Son bore.
He felt the crown of thorns upon his brow.
He heard the cries and blasphemies of his children.
He felt the tearing pain in his side.

Don't tell me God harmed his Son!
Don't tell me that he gave his Son as a sacrifice.
Don't tell me God was immune to the suffering.

Why! Because God was feeling everything too!

The only thing that God could not feel was sin!
But he felt his Sons' separation because of it.
He felt the loneliness and heartbrokenness of a father
He felt the darkness of death separate his child.

God wept. For his Son - was gone!

Even resurrections promise would not soothe his heart.
God's word had said that there had to be the perfect sacrifice.
The cleansing of blood!

Heaven was hushed as sobbing wracked the skies.

The angels fell on their faces - perplexed!

They heard the Father cry!

Don't tell me that God is separated from US!
He isn't.
Look at the Son as he is back -
by the Fathers side.
Standing in glory!

Look at him as he gazes into -
His fathers eyes with love!

GAZE WITH HIM!

Roman Justice

What a bloody mess! What a horror, not a man anymore.
The face was pulverised, the eyes blackened, the beard pulled.
If that was not enough - spittle on the face, as a scalding balm!
Screams and obscenities driven through the ears with minds of hate.
What a bloody mess - but it's only just started!

The feet and legs were forced wide and hands were tied aloft.
Now it gets interesting - now it gets legal - now for vengeance!
One to thirty-nine strikes - they all felt like one - like fire!
Blood pouring from his nose - his ear drums burst - vessels ruptured.
What a bloody mess - it's barely started - just a prelude.

Not only nearly blinded by his-own blood - deafened as well.
His pulse reached boiling point - his head would burst!
"Let's take him to be tried - a higher court - a good choice."
A Roman and his lackey were the best - justice blinded!
What a parade - what a scramble - only a short time left.

The hands were rung by Herod - what would he do - curiosity?
He moved around his quarry - silk covering his precious nose.
He didn't look dangerous - not now anyway - why worry?
Who could he send him to? A gift a new delight.
Returned at a slower pace - a bigger crowd - procurators law.

What a bloody mess.

"You again - I'd got rid of you!
You said you were 'Truth' - better than Caesar - little man!
Look at you now – alone - no one your champion.
No time to fight for you!"

The water bowl is lifted. Two bloodied hands -
clean washed - appeasements choice.

This is getting monotonous - reports are always boring.
Best to finish this tonight "More wine! More wine!"
Caesar clapped his hands - turned to the last part.
Let me see how Roman justice changes history - mine!
'Then dragged away to a gory death' ...... "I'll see it banned one day!"

The Caesar in Rome rested comfortably and yawned.
All was at peace with the world – his rule forever!
"Bah! What a bloody farce!
We couldn't let a pauper rule the world - COULD WE!"

Full Stop

The old man by the fountain sat - his arms were hung down low.
He gazed into the distant plain - his dreams had melt like snow.
What did he seek that led him here - the master of his life?
The mentors he had in his mind - had only given strife.

He had arrived life's end was near - his head was full of woe.
His crooked hands and shaking limbs - his movements now too slow.
What a course his life had been - he'd followed every path.
His knowledge he had increased - his search for truth a farce.

"What have you come here for?"- a voice cried out like rain.
The man replied - his voice was quiet - "To only ease my pain –
But water does not trickle here - my heart and soul is dry.
The sun it beats upon my brow - my accuser in the sky!"

"Lift up your hand and drink."- The voice went on to say.
"Look there's water from the spout - a bounty on the way."
"My dignity!" The man replied. "I will not stoop so low."
"Well! - that you will not have at all - in the life below!"

"The sun shall strike you down with heat and dust - be gone!"
"No!" said the man - "I want to change. I will not be alone!
Is it too late to change my ways - my errors to describe?"
The voice said that "Time is stopped! The future put aside."

He stumbled as he rose his eyes were red with tears.
"You've stopped the time to die - the time of many years.
Please take my thirst - dry my eyes - my soul, my heart to drench.
I leave myself - at your will - my sins a recompense."

"I take your sin - of many hues!" the voice it next replied.
"For I have saved a place for you - as I've already died!"
The man with voice of praise - bent down to drink - to quench.
The colour turned his heart to fear, for it was deaths dark stench.

The old man drank - and felt relief, for joy had compassed him.
"See your course!" The voice replied, "Was stained by all your sin!"
The old man stood, his back was straight - youth permeated limbs.
His strength renewed. His trust rescued - as he entered in.

The man began to pass the gate, his thoughts of older times.
Of those who searched, just like he did. Who saves them from their crimes?
He stopped - his thoughts of those below, was etched upon his brow.
"Dear voice! What can be done? Who will tell them now?"

"I will tell them how to drink - how to be renewed.
How to sacrifice their lives, and give themselves to God!
For 'I AM .' voice eternal, that speaks to all who hear.
Do not be sad! Lift up your soul, be joyful and good cheer."

"My name is SPIRIT!" The voice then cried. "I move upon the earth!
My purpose now is magnified - to give mankind new birth.
My sacrifice it was complete, turned life from tragedy.
My work was founded on my blood, all spilled at Calvary!

Praise to my father for the plan, the work is all begun.
My soul, my life has been spilled, for I'm his only Son!"
At last the man was satisfied, he laughed, and sang a song.
Of hopes and dreams, and wondrous things. Of righting of all wrongs.

Of people healed, and strength restored, of life beyond the veil.
Of beauty in a person's soul, of light, of depth all sealed.
He longed to go the way ahead, his stride it now was long.
The spirit nods for him to go, repeats eternals song.

In heaven, all glorious refrain - and it will repeat.
The chorus sung by men on Earth, is now in fact complete!
All praise the Fathers, eternal plan, men rescued from the abyss.
The Spirit touched the mans face, and said goodbye - a kiss!

He plunged to earth, a cry he made. His work to hurry on.
The song of hope, and joy, and love - goes on and on and won!
"Sing loud - sing high - sing soft - sing sweet, all voices sing aloud.
For life's worth more o'race of man, his victory does abound."

"Come one. Come all!" The Spirit cries, it moves upon the earth.
"All men of wisdom, and of sighs, do comprehend new birth.
See how the man, he changed his ways, his sin all washed away.
For he could not even pay the price, but only to obey!"

The Spirit rose to heaven's gate - he said "Let them come in!
The halt the lame, the sinners plain - them all to now begin.
The life's that's new, the life so true, the ancient plan of old
The story of our God made man - the story told and told!

Believe that life can be renewed - you need not stay forlorn.
For ready is the life for you - when you will be reborn!
Open your mouth and drink the blood - the spirit and the life.
For this decreed of God - The way-out, of all your strife!

Lift up your eyes, look here I come! My arms are open wide.
At last, at last the men of Earth - are taken as a prize!"
"It's finished now!" The Spirit cries - the blood flows like a river.
The men of faith are cleaned at last - and bounty in the quiver.

Children one, and children all, are gathered at the site.
The fountain now bears the name - 'The One of my delight!'
To never stop or run dry. Dark parched the earth to be.
Refreshment from the fountain's side is opened up - BY ME!

Eternal life - as source now - free for all made new.
Praise to the one whose plans complete - the dreams have all come true.
For man is reconciled to God - and to 'I AM' - they run.
The old man turned to youth was made - and 'I AM' - all the sum.

Epilogue

I was the man, the one who drank, and all my needs fulfilled.
To life's eternal plan I turned - because the Son was killed.
Alas my story now complete - my pen has all run dry.
The fountain calls me to my feet - and I must each day die!

The stories told - the stories done - it's passed from age to age.
The writer having write - is done - and now don't turn the page.
The thoughts are stilled - the story told - and now complete and true.
So now I close the book - and say - "ADIEU ADIEU ADIEU!"

98

STUDY GUIDE for BOOK 1

There are many themes in my poetry that overlap and repeat, sometimes from a different point of view.
I have kept the study in small 'bites' so that you can dip in and ponder in a relaxed way. The bible verses may not always mirror exactly the sentiments but I have endeavoured to make your time here interesting.

Study 1
1Child Within.

They say that when you drink alcohol to a certain level inhibitions are then shed. What comes out is usually a very noisy child or someone being especially mushy. Allowing the usual emotions that are hidden, to be let out. Unfortunately the person afflicted does not remember. And has only a bad headache constantly apologizes to their audience. Tragically negative emotions that had been hidden 'successfully' - spill out and can lead to destruction and violence. What a tragedy! A secret life can be! Remember God knows you in the secret place.

Study 2
2 Don't get wet. 14 Life's Solution. 20 Curiosity. 22 Weep in the dark place. 25 In a box. 29 Today.

Self preservation is a very strong instinct, it can be very good for us or it can be detrimental to our health. We can protect ourselves so much that we cannot 'belong'. When I was very young I had swimming lessons. Everyone else seemed to progress quickly, but I was afraid of lifting my feet from the floor of the pool. So I cheated! I was a tall child so I was able to 'swim' with my arms and bend down to water level, but kept my feet on the floor. It looked very good. I was 'swimming'. The trouble was I wasn't. My teacher expected me to 'swim' in deep water, 'oops!' I was found out and felt a fool. I was totally terrified as I screamed the place down. I can just about swim now, but I still hate deep water. I will swim to save my life, but I will never totally enjoy what looks so good. Fear of the unknown is a killer. Let him look into your soul. He will support you in everything. Listen to the 'Teacher', trust Him! I hope and pray that you don't get caught out.

Study 3
4 Open Wide. 15 The Invitation. 16 Plaster Saint.

The call for today is 'me me me' but how lonely it that phrase. How high do you place yourself? Are you jealous of others with different gifts or talents from you? Are you the centre of the universe? Imagine 'us us us' instead. Imagine borders being lost between a young and old, rich and poor, the haves and have not's. Imagine that all, become as a 'whole.' But still special, still chosen, still heard. I wonder what we could really accomplish. Would there then be 'plenty' for everyone, no-one left out or in need, but each belonging. Who is going to start this idea rolling or has it started already?

Study 4
6 The Lady and the Tramp. 9 Heir Apparent. 21 Top Dog.
68 At Any Price?

Man burrows into the depths of the earth to search for riches, small nuggets, and small glimmers of light - hidden for centuries. He sells his soul for dust from the earth but where does he end up. That's right the dust of the earth! What is important to you? What do you diligently search for? What is important to God. What and how much is He prepared to pay for it? How deep will He dig to reach it?

Study 5
3 Reflections. 7 Masque Parade.

Whatever the amount in currency you have in, 'millions' perhaps. Billions is spent and made in the cosmetic industry. We not only spend extravagantly on beautifying ourselves but also spend high sums on personal adornment. Your hidden nature is not really hidden! It is seen in all its glory by God. What parts are you afraid of? God has a plan for your redemption from you nature, a plan for change.

Study 6
8 Voices.

People can be so dogmatic that they have no heart for what they believe. They are such winners that others cower under their views, opinions and dogma. 'They are right and you are wrong!' We need wisdom and peace to know the truth.

Study 7
13 The Meeting. 79 Well Well Well.

This is one of the most intimate passages in the Bible. The Samaritan woman's meeting with the holy Jew, the one who was to pay the price for her. This can be experienced by all of us, but we don't go to the well head do we!

Study 8
19 Hooked.

We never know what someone is going through, what internal battle rages, what secrets darken the soul. We assume, with psychological tricks, that we can diagnose the reason. The reason why they act so 'wrong'. Remember 'Jobs' comforters', they tried to reason the escape route to a deeply troubled soul. The ultimate reality is we don't know the whole truth. Even the sufferer may not know everything, but 'thank God' for God - as He is!

Study 9
21 Top Dog.

Everyone has values; it's just that everyone's values are not the same! We all think we are right; we stick to it like glue, even when proved wrong! Some sensible ones know that they can be wrong. They are prepared to change their ways and opinions. Unfortunately some try to push their values or opinions on others with force or violence! A short cut. How powerful the ego is until a stronger ego overpowers them. Bullies are usually crushed by the victim, not because they fight back, but by them not coming under their power. Not becoming afraid. We are all experts at being wrong. What's your opinion?

Study 10
23 Plastic Surgery.

This is an avaricious age, an age of acquiring, an age of obtaining happiness in a bottle or a box. We acquire a lot from our past, but is it all good. The other angle is what do we waste our money on? What is used, and what just gathers dust! How many clothes in your cupboard? c.d's un-played, books unread clutter up your home. Did they do any lasting good? The merry-go-round of need, supply, sale, profit, and reinvention goes on and on. What would happen if it stopped and life was simpler? It never stops because there will be a 'new' thing next week. Next week may not come. What are you left with if at all disappears? What is real?

Study 11
24 Get Warmed.

The best relationships are two-way. When they become one-sided they cannot grow. They can change, but not for the better. What shifts and moves them around can be circumstances that separate us physically. The greatest relationship we can have is not bound by time or space. Not by circumstance. It can be reignited just by a thought. A turn of mind. What if the 'other one' transcends even our distant dark thoughts? The 'other' wants a relationship anyway. How would 'they' get through the independence barrier?

Study 12
26 The Visitor. 28 Do It Now. 43 Unnoticed.

The English eccentric Quentin Crisp once said about housework "Dusting need not be done because after 5 years it does not get any thicker." I expect some people use this wisdom as an excuse for not dusting. The trouble with dust is, it shows where you've been in the past. Everyone can see the trail! Dust does not
stop falling, it just gets more weighed down and the illusion is created. Sin is like this, just because you can't see it, it does not mean it's not there! Just by thinking something does not make it true. Get your duster out, get to work every day. Don't let sin, pain and sorrow live with you. Go to the cleansing place. The Cross. That's my theory anyway. I wonder what it would be like if windows were opened on a windy day, or do we sit in the fug! Your choice.

Study 13
27 Propagation.

Plants grow when they are properly nurtured, watered and given light and nutrients. I have a lot of plants that are in various stages of growth from blooming magnificently. To turning yellow stage when I have either over watered or over exposed the plant to sunlight. Built into each plant is the design map that states how to grow. What sort of soil what amount of water is necessary to thrive. Try and grow potatoes up poles like green beans. Or roses in shallow pots, with only the air to feed it. The key to growth is inside all of us. Follow the pattern in a holy way and you will thrive and produce fruit and you will also be yourself.

Study 14
30 Take Eat.

The bug-bear many of us have is the motivation to pray or to read the bible. Not just motivation but the lack of hunger. I went back to my childhood when fresh bread was delivered at the door and the hunger it caused. It was difficult not to break off a corner and eat. Enjoy it!

Study 15
33 When You Pray. 37 Silence in Court. 57 Listening One.

Our souls twist and turn when we pray. We become guilty when our selfishness interrupts our thoughts. We are supposed to be holy when we pray not carnal. How many times you do you feel you have failed. This is the normal way of the soul we battle against our nature, we always will! The solution is how much we follow our basic nature. It needs a turn of the head a signpost showing the way. The correct way to follow is covered with stones and thorns, but the destination lies ahead, it is glorious! The most important thing to remember is that prayer is a two-way street – you are not talking to yourself! He listens and talks back but we do not always hear Him. The Son also prays for us. He has the Fathers ear. He speaks for us!

Study 16
34 Scapegoat.

There is a ceremony in the Jewish year that culminates in the sins of the people being laid on the back of the 'scapegoat'. The sins are taken by the goat out into the wilderness. The plan of God was different from this poem but sin is a reality. It is suffered by all of us. It is never too late, even the point of death, if you turn, can be a starting place. Remember the two thieves.

Study 17
35 The Sentence Is!

Some people are born dancers some are not. The worst is when you love dancing but have two left feet. They trip you up, but still you dance and twirl. The only dancing you have is in your head. It becomes a dream. Which is reality? The real body dancing or the dream body dancing. That's what 'grace' is like. The reality of it exists in itself. We can give our own reality to it, or live in a dream and not fully understand it. Grace is born from God not out of creation at all - and if it's of God; - it's eternal. No thinking or dreaming will change or stop it.

Study 18
36 Fashion Statement. 42 Thought Police.

The glossy magazines shine at us. The messages of renewal, revamping, reinventing is a common theme. The next month the design has changed. There is no stability in what is peddled, no depth at all. What sort of show do you front to the world? What really makes you tick. What is below the surface? Are you base metal and not gold. What is the price you pay to keep up the pretence? What is the price you pay for the truth?

Study 19
39 Look this Way.

It's said that science is the new religion, that God is dead. As the years progress the idea that science is the ultimate thing is failing. Faith in the 'evolution' principle – or theory is now diminishing more and more. Why? Because of the miracle in creation of 'everything' being just right or in total balance. If only one thing increased, for instance too much oxygen, then plants die. If plants die man and animals die. This because one system has become out of balance and order. It takes faith to believe in evolution – a lot of faith. There is another reality all around us. Think on that.

Study 20
40 Constancy.

Who can we trust anymore? We read biased newspaper articles and watch "skewed" TV broadcasts. We trust the manufactures of food that the healthy label they highlight for us is true. The hidden salt and fat is just not magnified, not an issue. Who can we trust anymore! We live on slippery ground and wish that we had a strong foothold. Even gravity is against us. At some point we have to peak around the barrier erected to protect us and hope that "this is someone I can trust." It's more than a shame that we are disappointed; more – that we are delighted by the reality we find. What is the only reality? Let's see!

Study 22
41 Christmas Cheer. 48 Broken Dreams.

There is a saying 'familiarity breeds contempt'. This is a saying that can suck the life out of relationships, marriages, fellowship and also from the soul! So much is open to us but we have become blunted by life itself and so life becomes 'dull'. We also expect too much from people, that they are unable to give! We forget sometimes that life is being renewed and reinvigorated every day. A child picks up a classic fairy tale and for the first time it's read they are enthralled. The imagination of the child takes them on a journey even when repeated for the umpteenth-time. The journey is always new and fresh. This happens every day but to the child it's new. Keep your childhood alive see things, the old familiar things, new again because it is!

Study 22
44 Broken Reed. 88 The Good Shepherd.

You've learnt all the verses and passages from 'His word'. Nothing can harm you, be upbeat in life. But what if good thoughts don't protect. Tragedy happens. Sickness appears. His 'Word' says 'goodness and mercy shall follow me all the days of my life?' Does this mean no negatives! Does this mean God lied? How do we live through negatives, by living in the positives?

When Christ was being whipped, humiliated, tortured and reviled what was on His mind. I think some of His thoughts were 'I forgive them! I love them! I obey you Father! This is for your glory!' These are the verses we should remember! There is pain as well as healing and joy on the path we all must tread.

Study 23
46 I Was There.

Our minds can decide who our enemies are even without proof. We all have enough imagination for that! Usually our feelings have been hurt – they make the decision for us! OUCH!

Study 24
47 Longing Heart. 62 Always the Same. 70 Greatest Make-Over.

Gods love for sinners is overwhelming! How much did his heart burn for us. He sent the perfect sacrifice. His Son volunteered to give his all. Their hearts burst in their love for us. The Holy Spirit spread his wings around the Earth in redemptive love. He came down for us all. Listen to his heartbeat, He wants to give all.

Study 25
11 Closeness. 49 Mellow Meadow. 61 Dark and Light.

The world and life spins far too fast for most of us. A secret place to "chill out" just for a little while is a reality for some, but impossible for many. Just a breath. A breathing space, a time out is wonderful and ordained by God Himself. You don't have to be perfect or ready to visit this place. Even pain is welcomed here. Keep the 'Sabbath', the day of rest. Rest like I do says the King of the universe. This answer is better than popping pills, better than drinking to oblivion, or even than a real cup of tea! Just sit back, close your eyes and enjoy!

Study 26
50 Balancing Act. 59 Foundation. 72 Time Waster. 82 Living Life.
83 Crunch Time.

Can you ride a bike? Its great fun to 'whoosh' down a hill with your feet off the peddles, the wind rushing past your ears. You can't do this the first time you sit on a bike, if you tried you would fall off. It takes time to get it right. Is your life a 'a rush and tear'. A constantly chasing your tail never getting anything done on time or leaning to much on one task and never completing the most important one. You are suffering from 'hurry sickness!' You are out of balance. Some people even gloat when you wobble and fall. Our master and teacher
never rushed anywhere. There is time in every day for everything that really needs to be done. Don't make an excuse for inactivity. You may regret it!

Study 27
58 Word Power.

We are bombarded by opinions and thoughts from the media. Not just visually but verbally. There can be such a noise that quietness is never felt. This is about the power of words, for good as well as for evil. They cut to the soul and quick of each one of us. What type of 'words' do you read?

Study 28
63 All Chosen. 65 The Misunderstanding. 69 Together.

What is your God like, how do you see him? I hope this picture helps you destroy the negative thoughts you have about him. God said "I AM that which I AM!" and that is his name as well as his nature. He cannot be changed by our opinions or the thoughts of others. he is as 'He' is!

Study 29
64 Prove It.

We all want everything sown up and have complete knowledge of everything. Faith is impossible for us. This poem speaks of what God has done! It needs no faith to understand it. The best understanding is in the last line. He has the last line anyway!

Study 30
69 Together.

I recently met a financial consultant whose task it was to build up a framework for my financial future regarding pension etc. He uses probabilities and possibilities in his calculations. He had to balance the costs to the company and project possibilities in the future that would affect the value of the package. Both 'sides' are supposed to 'win'. As more varied situations are put into the equation the accuracy diminishes. I wonder how God planned 'salvation'. How he made it a benefit to both 'sides'. I like his solution. Don't you!

Study 31
75 Home Life.

There was a discussion on the radio about the incarnation of God. The fact that God became, in Jesus, not only wholly God, but wholly man! I felt that this must have been a huge shock for Jesus to find himself in human form, but what a real-person he became for us! He experienced everything that we do. Check out 'the gospels' and find a new picture of what the 'Christ' is really like.

Study 32
6 The Lady and the Tramp. 81 The Sleeper.

I wonder how many people have stood in front of the 'Mona Lisa' and wondered what she is thinking or smiling about? Imagination could run riot with the idea that she has a secret love, or just won the lottery! Is she dreaming about all the wonderful dresses, jewellery, cakes that she can now afford? Imagination is used by actors in their portrayal of characters that are not in 'our imagination'. Making their character come to life but only in how the actor sees them. How he has judged them to be. Enjoy your imagination. What a gift.

Study 33
76 Woodwork. 78 The Leader.

The most popular and well known psalm is no 23, 'The Lords my shepherd'.
It encapsulates all the outworking of the gospel in a few short words. The closeness is apparent; but to touch the sheep? Talk to the sheep? Inspect the sheep? These are not shown, but he does it anyway. Why does he touch the sheep? To find sickness and injury, yes! But what happens to the whole sheep?. 'Sacrifice!' That's what! The sheep without blemish 'died' on the altar. They were sacrificed daily in the temple. He knew that; when he chose each one! He was glad that they were whole. And glad that they were worthy!

Study 34
59 Foundation. 81 The Sleeper.

The first line of an old song states, 'He's got the whole world in his hands' – perhaps we should sing it when we wake up! Everything is under his protection and love; we are totally dependent on him for everything, and even his judgement! Why be happy about that! Because he is righteous and just. God does not wear gloves to stop being tainted by this world. His hands have become dirty with the sins of the world. They are ingrained with our destiny because we are written there. How big are his hands? Larger than the universe and yet his thumb gently grips us close to his heart. He is in control.

Study 35
84 Triumphant Entry.

We've heard the message of the gospel from many sources and we are positive we know the story inside out. That there is nothing new to hear. Sometimes our ears need opening so we hear properly. We should not jump to the credits of a film first. We should be surprised who stars in the film and say, 'It did not look like him, or sound like him. What an actor!' We applause. How many people 'act' their days-away. Can we see behind the 'deception'. Can we lift the veil to see reality. Do we judge when it is not our job to 'judge'. What scriptwriter do you follow. Don't applause the deceiver. Applause the 'Word of God'.

Study 36
86 Servant-hood. 87 What a Mistake.

Hero's should always be head and shoulders above others. They should be handsome and charismatic, they should topple tyrants. Well that's the world's perspective. God's perspective is from the other end of the telescope. He came as a Jew, a despised race. No description carved in stone to show his beauty or stature. He got his hands grubby with the sins of the world, like a gardener He bent down. He became one of us!

Study 37
91 Imagine.

There is a saying that you should not judge anyone until you have walked in their shoes. Other peoples walk looks easy or even insignificant, until we experience the same thing. What would it be like if we kept the other persons life and could not give it back! Could not shake of the unimaginable. It becomes our property, our reality. I don't think many would choose that path. Do you?

Study 38
9 Heir Apparent.94 Roman Justice.

How far will you go to prevent something that you know will happen! If you knew a child would be a 'Hitler' would you 'get rid' of him before he was born?
Fear and pride lashes out in many guises to deal with 'problem children'. Lock them up! Don't let them exist! Don't feed them anymore!. All these logically thought out, very humane! Just a short sharp shock that will do the trick. Turn the tide! But does the tide bring water you need, or does it drown you? History repeats itself! But God will not repeat 'redemptions' solution. There was a 'short- sharp- shock' to the kingdom of darkness, but it blazed out to 'eternity!'
Don't let your time pass without confronting the kingdom of 'light'. Don't sweep the plan of God under the carpet. You could be killing the wrong thing!

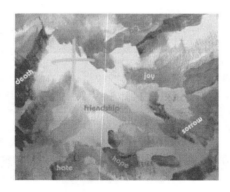

Holy Bible References

The Holy Bible is full of people who struggle with pain, uncontrolled emotions, situations and circumstances that cripple them. I have enclosed a few examples to get your mouth watering and make you see that 'you are not alone'. I have included verses about God and Jesus and the Holy Spirit so you will also recognize that GOD is not a far away entity – but has emotions like us. Remember He made us like Him! God bless you.

MAN'S NATURE

Avarice	Luke	12	vs	13-21
Greed	Matthew	6	vs	19-24
	Joshua	17	vs	14-21
Bereavement	Genesis	37	vs	34-35
	Genesis	50	vs	1-4
Conspiracy	Genesis	37	vs	18-31
Duplicity	Proverbs	11	vs	3
Critical	Matthew	7	vs	1-5
Bitterness/Hate	Genesis	37	vs	3-8
Afraid	Matthew	8	vs	24-27
	Matthew	10	vs	26-30
Drunkenness	Genesis	9	vs	20-24
	1 Samuel	25	vs	36-37
Jealousy	Numbers	12	vs	1-2
Tempted	Genesis	39	vs	7-20
Accused	Genesis	42	vs	9-14
Helpless	Psalm	30	vs	10-12
	Psalm	101	vs	1-2
Uncertain	Daniel	3	vs	16-18
Double-minded	Proverbs	4	vs	14
Fear	Genesis	9	vs	27
Disaster	Jeremiah	9	vs	1-2
	Obadiah	1	vs	12-14
	Ezekiel	14	vs	22
Undisciplined	Proverbs	10	vs	17
Troubled	Psalm	142	vs	1-7
Protection	Psalm	140	vs	1-8
Friendship	Psalm	133	vs	1
Free of Guilt	Isaiah	59	vs	20
	Isaiah	59	vs	15-16
Peacekeeper	Genesis	50	vs	19-21
Short Lived	Psalm	103	vs	15-16

GOD'S NATURE

Anger	Mark	11	vs	15-17
	Jeremiah	10	vs	10
	1 Kings	11	vs	9
Weeps	John	11	vs	35
Troubled	John	12	vs	27
Calls Out	Isaiah	5	vs	26
Loves Totally	Matthew	23	vs	37
Restorer	Amos	9	vs	11
	Isaiah	49	vs	21-27
Reconciler	2 Corinthians	5	vs	18-21
	Hosea	3	vs	1
Generous	Luke	9	vs	16-17
	Nehemiah	9	vs	20-25
Self-less	Ephesians	5	vs	2
	John	10	vs	11-18
	Isaiah	53	vs	1-12
	Hebrews	10	vs	5-10
Compassionate	Isaiah	54	vs	8
	Psalm	103	vs	8-22
Kind	Isaiah	30	vs	19-26
Provider	Psalm	23	vs	1-6
Protector	Psalm	23	vs	4
Rewarder	Revelation	22	vs	12-17
Displeased	Isaiah	59	vs	15-16
Just	Deuteronomy	32	vs	4
Time Manager	John	2	vs	4
Hates	Proverbs	6	vs	16-19
Loves Forever	Psalm	103	vs	17
Judge	Ezekiel	14	vs	21-23
Intervener	Isaiah	59	vs	16-21

BOOK 2

Cash in your Chips

Life's a gamble we all have a high stake. Ourselves!
The value of our lives is placed on the altar of self.
This altar is tall and wide but easy to climb.
Its sides are a gentle slope reachable by all.

We carry all our best in our arms and sow it gratefully.
What bounty! What interest do we get from our offering?
We get self-back not just from ourselves but others.

Our riches are tarnished and torn are scattered and fall.
Our riches once glowed when our hearts were gold -
but now our currency has become dross.

We had followed the advice of professionals, life gurus, media.
Our ears had been tickled by the prospect of gain and interest.
But poverty is in our souls even as we are silk clad.
Our labels have been chosen .The fashion of today.
Our minds have been bent to serve self not others.

The bid had been placed the wheel was spun. The ball fell.
This choice in a spin of a wheel has trapped us.
We go again and again to the 'bank of self" it must payout!
There must be an interest payment soon! Better than loss!

We seek and gamble and prosper in this world but our souls die.
Our souls were of great value once now we only grab and take.
The treasure trove has been buried and covered.
We mark the spot on the map and hide with a code.

We bury those who should have gained by our true wealth.
The wealth and bounty that had been bought by 'The Son'!
But we would not cash in - deposit or redeem our souls.
We are left to be dust underfoot and not 'Glory gold'.

Embryo

Don't breathe be very still. Do not exhale.
Hold your breath don't be heard or seen.
Hold tight knuckle-ride this day out.

Let your heart be still and quiet.
Hold still. Do not breathe or your dreams will fly.
They will go up in dust and cloud. Lost forever.

Don't hold onto your dreams the cynic says.
The cynics smiles and has a wise look.
You believe them and hold tight.
The little promise the little seed ready to plant.
Nestled in your heart by the gardener - the answer of all.

You felt joy when the idea the dream the vision –
was captured by the soil in your heart.
You watered it, nestled it like a baby.
But this seed was so small like dust.
Only a wet finger could pick it up and place inwardly.

The gardener licked, and guided the little life.
The new promise.
It was placed perfectly.

But the poison and harsh wind blew across your heart.
You believed that nothing could grow.
You have inside you the 'Holy Seed' the 'True Vine'.
Don't listen to the wind.
Listen carefully.

The shoot is now pushing, pushing the words to the light.
It contains life and blooms.

The Stain

Its spring!

I've got the broom handy. The energy needed.
I have left everything through the winter.
I have left basic chores to do 'my own thing'.
The glorious sun now shines and glows on -
shows the infinite dust and clutter.

I bought bits, books and wonderful things to brighten.
They looked good in the brightly lit shop.
They never look the same at home. Do they?

I stand with my broom and a wet cloth in my hand.
What do I do first? I was never organized.
I remember how long last year took.
I went at it hammer and tongs, cleaning, moving, stacking.
But I did so much and what was I left with?
I was left with a different mess.

I had no system, no plan, just got on with it.
I had no thought, no strategy to get my house in order.
My head hurts. I remembered.
I had ended up with more chaos, not less.

I stood in the corner and wept over my feet.
It seemed so futile.
An idea - a fleeting thought - came to me.
'Clean your feet'. So I did!
Then 'Clean the space around your feet'.
So I did!
Then 'Clean the next space'.

My heart was not heavy anymore.
I was succeeding without trying.
A lesson for all cleaners!

Start now!

115

Late Bloom

All the other flowers had bloomed and blossomed.
They had lifted up their heads and caught the sun.
They had basked in the heat and the glorious light.
They had turned their heads towards the source.
They had reached maturity and then started to fade.
They had to fade and die. Had to create seed.

They had to go through the process to be a sacrifice.
They fell to the ground as a seed pod a seed head.
They cracked open, spilled out and sank.
They sank into the darkness and were gone.

I was still stretching for the sky for the heavens.
I had always been slow always behind others.
I creaked and groaned. I was getting over stretched.

My body was becoming tired of growing.
It was tired of always striving waiting for finality.
I was late bloomer. A slow budding an un-cast seed.
I was nearly left on the back burner.
Others had flamed.
A late bloomer: a slow grower - perennial

I really thought I was nothing while others grow.
Others had a harvest - a crop - a bounty.
I forgot that there is a season for every purpose.
A time to live and a time to die!
A time to grow fruit and a time to blossom.
A late bloomer.
Yes.
But I am meant to be this.
I am fulfilling my harvest.
Amen.

116

Money Management.

I will spend when my bank balance is full!
I will spend and give when I owe no one.
Not a penny will I spend on myself or others.
I will get out of debt. I will be flush and full.

This had gone on for too long, that poverty was mine!
Poverty was a gift I had opened years ago.
I struggled with payments for useless things.
Then I struggled to pay for shelter and food.
Money slipped through fingers like water.
It poured away and evaporated.

Others gave me gifts and vouchers and cheques.
Get balanced get sorted. This will do it for you.
The sums never matched. The loss increased.
I was spiraling into the abyss of debt.

It smothered, covered and drowned me.
I fought valiantly and hard.
My goal was to be able to look others in the eyes.
To say I will pay this bill. I will supply your need.
But I was always poor. Always owing.
My mind whirled over these problems.
I never connected and never loved or spent my heart.

Why was that? The reason I was poor?
I never withdrew from the bank God supplies.
It is full of love and credit is free.
I never opened the account that has my number on it.

Never rich - me!

Buy Me!

"Do you have a catalogue please?"
I asked the agent on the line.
I need to see all that you supply so I can choose.

I waited expectantly for the 'plop' on the mat, it arrived.

I opened up the wrapper and gazed at the cover.
Brilliantly coloured, highlighted offers blazed to me.
Starred bargains were shown on each page.
Buy this. Buy me. Offer of the month.
The pages were packed from top to bottom.
All the necessities of life were in this book.

I showed my neighbours and friends the pages.
They were envious and wanted to buy as well.
We even had a special gathering together.
A bargain 'bulk purchases' was our plan.
Each one handed over a list of purchases.

They knew that the costs would be high so some borrowed.
They paid by plastic was the plan.
So many things were bought that we rejoiced.
We knew that all our needs would come soon.

We added the number of items and turned to the book again.
The last pages were opened, the prices checked.
There was no price, no inventory, no charge.

The last page stated in bold letters
NO CHARGE!

We had been told the cost was high.
It was very high but not ours!
NO PAYMENT. NO GAIN.

AMEN!

Choice Words

Choose your thoughts today.
Don't pick off the shelf the out of date thought.
The dented tins the end of line products.
Don't get cheap bargains, the easy way.
Thoughts for sale 'Buy one get free'.
What a laugh you are NOT free.

Your mind whirls. The words ricochet from the minds' walls.
Your mind is crowded with 'special offer' of today.
I don't like them. I hate those types. I hate happiness.
Choose your thoughts today.

You bought your credit card; the account was full but so what.
Why bother to get my act together. I chose what I want.
I say choose your thoughts today.

Even this bargain is crowded with good and bad.
It cries from the choices, the goodies, the mess.
Choose your thoughts today.
There is such a clatter, chatter. A noise.
There is such junk, such sound, such deceit, such garbage.
Choose your thoughts today.

I am trying. I am fighting. I am beating myself.
I am beating my brow, wracking my brain, my way.
It does not work!
Choose your thoughts today.
New thoughts, pure thoughts.

There will be no room for garbage, fear, hate and spite.
There will be no room for sorrow, jealousy and denial.
There will only be room for 'My thoughts'.
Holy pure clean.
Joyous peaceful and healing!
Choose! Choose! Choose!

119

Spent

Just a little coin rattling in the tin.
Just a small gift of everything - and nothing left.
The coin nestled in amongst others coloured gold and silver.
They were worth so much more and grand design.
They were also showing the face of the king, the stamp.
The stamp of authority and who the worth belonged to.

The little coin was gathered up and slid through fingers.
It fell back into the treasure as it could not be held.
It was insignificant and feeble a sorry sight.
So small.
But this little coin had been given in love.

It could purchase hearts and joy and worth.
It was multiplied many times over.
It was and became - worth more than face value.

Why did this happen?

Because a pauper did not count the cost of worship.

This pauper reached into their heart and spent themselves.
The story of this little coin shines above treasures.
It shines above the glitz and glory of the bulk.

It has always been shown as the valued coin.
The coin spent totality to Gods glory.
The coin was turned in God's hand.
And his son's face shone back.
God currency is priceless and indestructible!

Mosaic

The little pieces of red, blue and gold are ready.
They are small pieces with a destiny.
Each one is individual unique and beautiful.

They are made from earth's clay.
Moulded in hands of an artist.
The master craftsman slapped the clay.
A resounding sound and then the cutting.
The cutting and shaping.

The clay had been baked and coated.
The paints and enamel fired red hot.
Little points of light shine on the sharp edges.

They were clipped and shuffled.
Sorted, none discarded.
Broken ones kept in a special box.

They were getting ready to be assembled.
Assembled into God's pattern and design.

The lost broken pieces carefully matched.
They drew close to each other and united.
All were united in a wonderful mosaic.
Each piece was a hurt feeling, pride or pain -
Suffering torment shame and doubt.

Nothing was lost.
All renewed, and reused.
The glorious image of the soul set free.
Complete and radiant.

A bridal picture beckons.
AMEN.

Heir Apparent

"At last he has gone!"

One space left at the table.
Now empty. Now incomplete.
He has gone out into the world.
"Good riddance I say!
He was a pain!"

I woke one morning, a smile on my face.
Another day of duty and morality and law.
I am a hard worker. I always had been.
I never shirk my duty to my father.

'Not like him - The runaway, the scrounger'.

I bent over the plough adjusting the ropes.
The ground was dry today but clouds filled the sky.
Rain would be on the field soon.
A harvest in the future.

I pushed the plough into the softening earth.
Always ready to work - a dutiful son.
The sun had beat on my head all day.
I had organized the servants.
Gave out the rosters.
I was the 'bosses son'.
The elder governor.
The one who could order anyone to do my will.
The inheritance had been divided.
I had my share.

But I was a dutiful son. I ploughed my furrow.
My duty was my purpose in my life. My head was high.

Suddenly father yelled and ran to the gate.
Ran up the road and was gone.

I carried on my duty.
That was my purpose.
That was my law.

Nothing will move me today!

Pride and Prejudice.

What would you do to show that you loved them?
Would you return the bag with flowers, so girly?
To the owner who has vanished up the street.
Would you hide it and run to return secretly?

Your manly ego can be embarrassed by kindnesses.
What would you do to show that you love them?
Would you listen to the same story the third time -
-and laugh genuinely and with good humour.

Would you not let the older one know their repetition?
Would you keep them in that happiness and content?
Or would your pride snap and say 'enough'!

You are not shown by what you do but how you do it.
It takes a gentle loving heart to bathe beggar's feet.
But proud man buys another drink and turns away.
What would you do to show love?

Are you prepared to be judged as effeminate or a fool.
But by doing right and love another.
Are you prepared to be a simple fool listening to the old.
Someone who cannot tell the truth about the 'retelling tale'.

Are you prepared to bathe beggars' feet and look soft.
Your actions are all watched and judged by others.

Does their opinion matter to you.
Whose opinion should you be listening to anyway?

Body Image

I stood in front of the 'morph' mirror.
"How fat do you think you are" the voice said.
The image was tweaked and moved in and out.
My hips grew, my stomach shrank.
The image was what I see.
"Stop! That's me. That's my size!"

The bulk, hulk moved off the mat.
I was huge. The mirror had confirmed it.
The nurse tapped her pen on the desk.
She wrote a note and sent me to the next stage.

"Breathe in the tube. Blow as hard as you can."
The apparatus obeyed my breath.
The pen soared and dipped at my pressure.
I must have been very sick. I needed rest.

The nurse moved me on to take blood.
This is the bit I never like.
Always painful.
The tests are all over. A report will be made.
We will see how fit you are.

I was very despondent as I knew I had not passed.
I was overweight, out of breath and weak.
"Go and get dressed. We have finished the assessment.
A slip of paper was proffered.

The report said.

HEALTHY fit for work.

Report to the desk.

Uniform provided.

Support always on hand.

WELCOME to the KINGDOM!

Cheap Cheep.

You are worth more than five sparrows.
You are never overlooked or forgotten.
You may feel like the dust, blown away and lost.

You disappeared into the vapours and are forgotten.

That is how you feel and how you are to men!

But God the beloved Father has bought you for a price.
You are the richest thing the richest one ever purchased.
You do not have shackles on your ankles and yoked neck.
You are not held in a gilded cage.

Why did he buy you? You say.
You are of no value.
You do not know that freedom has to be bought.
You have no pennies to hand over to the jailer.
To make your life more comfortable.

You are worth more than five sparrows.
The little birds were waiting for the release.
They still sing even though bars surround them.

You are worth more than five sparrows.
You may feel that you have dashed against the bars too often.
You have been damaged cannot fly, cannot sing.
You have no light in your eyes anymore.

You are worth more than five sparrows.
If they had been his treasured child.
Even God would have died for five sparrows.

Even they had sinned.

You are worth more than five sparrows.
Never forgotten, never lost, never worthless.

His always! SING!

126

Message in a Bottle.

The bottle in the sink accuses me.
It is a silent potent witness of my failure.
I grab the neck and throw it to the ground.
It smashed in a thousand pieces.

I wept into the water that was left too clean.
It was another witness that I was a filthy rag.
I was covered in grey and darkness.
I bit my jaw and tipped the water out.
It gurgled down the sink a horrible melody.
It accused, accused, accused.

I stood leaning on the sink for a timeless moment.
I did not feel anger or pain or sorrow.
Just, accused, accused, accused.

I lift my stained face to the window.
A wintry day, a blowing wild wind outside.
I don't even feel wild about myself.
I cannot change my heart my mind my soul.

My habit overrules me and laughs in the corner.
It accused, accused, accused.

I threw the dish rag in the sink and got splashed.
The final dregs of my life laughed at me.
Why am I like this I asked?
Why do I strive and never win the race.
I feel accused again.
Accused, accused, accused.

A bubble of soap hit my hand and glory was on it.
The colours of the rainbow.
He remembered me!
He will never destroy the same way!

The little rainbow gave me HOPE for today.
TODAY I am not accused!
AMEN!
I HAVE HOPE!

Face 2 Face.

Just because I am not beautiful,
does not mean I have an ugly soul!
Just because my face is pale and warped.
My eyes bulge and I cannot speak.
Does that mean 'I am nothing?

I don't look in mirrors lightly.
Others mirror my face!
I see the look in their eyes.
The sideways gasp.

I don't say much. I don't go to open places.
My home is the dark and lonely spaces.
I never make friends, never lunch or parties.
I am ostracized and outcast.

But someone looks my way.
I stop in my tracks and look to the floor.
I must escape the gaze.
This gaze is innocent and beautiful!
Beautiful blue eyed are looking straight at me.

The hand grasps upwards to reach my neck.
I struggle to bend to the level of the new friend.
The eyes sparkle and twinkle.
So small - so lovely.
The hands badly deformed by disease grasp as best they can.

I then notice the eyes cannot see.
The lips cannot speak.
The face of the child is innocent of my ugliness.
The deformed child gives me a hope I don't deserve.

A tear reaches my eyes and drops on his face.
The child laughs.
He has made a new friend too!

Just a Game!

Everything was set out and ready.
The pieces were in place, a level plain.
Everyone has the same chance.
Its just a few lucky ones will win!

The dice is thrown. Money invested and spent.
Properties, public services, goods and properties.
ALL need to make a profit.

The roll of the dice.
The turn of the screw.
A level plain! But not now!

The clever lucky ones crow and preen and demand!
RENT! PAYMENT! RESTITUTION!
Get out of the way!
Our improvement scheme needs money!

Cash is back handed and thrust into Swiss accounts.
Play gets dirty and the object of the game is not money, but power.

A level plain. Not now or ever again.
The poor get poorer, the rich increase.
They increase their land, their purses, their waists.
Money has a smell all its own.

Addiction is a wonderful thing when you win!
Banks get corrupted as well, secrets leak.
Friends slap on the back and put in the knife.
Shares are fought over and mud slung.
A level plain. Not anymore!

This is my time. The heap is mine.
The chips are going my way.

The timer pings! The people groan.
The GAME has ended.

The pieces are put back into the box.
The winner goes home.
See you next time.

Battle of Words

Call up the soldiers, bring in the troops.
I am overwhelmed and out numbered.
My arms are tired but I keep on fighting.
I call to the signaler 'blow the horn, call the troops'.
The trumpeter is overwhelmed by the foe but he blows.
He blows with his last breath, the call to arms.

The troops are sleeping in repose.
They had been on 'stand-down' for so long that they do not rouse quickly.
They stretched and yawned and blinked their eyes.
'The call. The call' they cried.
They rallied and scrambled grabbed spears and knives.
Their shields were left behind in their haste.
The battle was joined, the fight was on.

I turned and saw the melee, the jostle, the mess.
I heard the yelling, and orders, and scream of death.
The enemy was fighting hard.
It seemed to have the upper hands.
I called to arms again. But NO troops left.

We were a small band, a weak band but faithful.
We knew the cause we fought for and were made for.
Why had there not been more troops?
More on our side?
Because we had not fed our minds -
hearts and souls with the word.
We had allowed the enemy of lies to become truth to us.

Our battle plans had been re-drawn by out own hand.
What is written, what is read is what fights for us?
No 'God word' no 'Word of the Spirit' no back up plan.
We nearly lost because we would not take the time -
to remember our written orders.
Its in 'His word' in His book'.

We left it unopened and unused.
We should have obeyed and did not!

Point of Contact

It's a secure place that everyone knows.
The top of the stairs.
A place to hide and be seen.
A place that can give a secret view of the party.

It is also a place of pain and thirst.
When the cry 'I've got a tummy ache'.
Or 'I'm thirsty.' Eloquent, longing words.
The place is a site of warmth when mother answers.
Warm arms caress and kiss and say 'Get back to bed'.

But for some this place has to be quiet.
Not found out!
The punch and kick and screaming could start.
Don't breath too heavily they may hear.

Sometimes a glass of water is proffered and drunk.
Drink very slowly, getting hiccups.
Tears are wiped and eyes get sleepy.

This place is the same in every home.
A place of shelter or of panic and pain.
A place where there can be great love.
Or a place of coldness and joylessness.

But you only want to see, to feel and to belong.
Legs dangle through the bars.
You live in hope each time.
What will come up the stairs?
Joy or pain.

The steps grow bolder, bated breath then what.
What this time?

Who?

You are dry and hungry yet you fed on ashes.
The gurus and teachers leading you to light failed you.

Your heart so longed for enlightenment, peace, joy.
You were prepared to hang with hooks in your mouth
A sacrifice. A show of your dedication.

You joined the million throng - at the sacred river.
You plunged into the dirt the sacred flow.
You waited for the heart to be satisfied and filled.

Only a short glimpse a flicker of light touched you.
It gave a blessing with a sting in its tail.
The sting was!
"Try and reach me again. What sacrifice to reach me?"
You went deeper into the sacred words.
Your body twisted in praise.
You breathed the breath of the yogis.
You blotted out your eyes.
No sun reached your soul only futility.
You had gone the whole way waiting for oblivion.

Waiting for nirvana, enlightenment, nothingness.

But you found yourself all alone.
Not one hand could help you now.
Not one heart even beat for you.
You stood in the holy river waiting to die.
Nobody told you that someone had died for you!
Nobody cared or touched your shoulder.
You let go plunged into eternity.

Lost and gone............

Goodbye!

Limping Legs

"Run!" They said. "Run for that is the way to riches and bounty."

Run as fast as you can. Be smart be ahead
The pack is snapping at my heels.
Promotion! Promotion! Up the ladder
You will not reach me there
I am above you. I have authority and strength.
I pant and draw my breath. The race is won.
Hurrah 'king of the hill'.

It's a good view up here a long view
Above peoples heads
I see the grey and the bald
The hung low and the minions
I am the BOSS!

Then hands on. Control time.
I grip the bar and rule with a hand of steel.
I will ensure that the corporation will conquer.
I expect you are expecting me to fall
Well fool you!

I am stable and on a firm foundation.
My profit margin is calculated.
Beat all opposition
I am in the 'Top 100'.
Further, further and higher I go
You still think I will fall?
Your words choke me
You bring up bile in my chest
A sharp pain!

D d   d   d   d   d   d   d…………..……….!

The Avenger

'Run! Run! Pick up your feet and run.'
'Be swift! Go now! Get a move on! Run!'
My breath became short. My ribs ached and fell
My feet stumbled and twisted on the stones.
My ankles ached and shot with pain.

'Run run' was the cry. The dogs were after me.
I could hear the accusations in my ears
Baying for my blood. 'Run run.'

I panted and hung on to the tree and leaned for rest.
'Run run.' The dust sprang around me choking
My mind span and whirled - accusing and fainting.
'Why did this happen? How did I do such a thing?
'Run run!'

The stream was ahead of me and up the hill - sanctuary.
I waded waist deep willing my last ounce of breath.
It chilled my soul but I looked to safety.

The chaser got nearer. The avenger with sword held high.
I scrambled up the bank knuckles bled and torn.
My knees scarred and riven red.
Pulling myself up the cliff.
I climbed and raised - my hands and feet.
Long searched for footholds.

I fell at the entrance - the gates of sanctuary.
'Let me in. let me in, Sanctuary I claim.'

The soldiers and priests pulled open the doors.
I fell through the portal, worn weary and spent.
'Sanctuary!' I gasped as water was offered.
I drank. I gazed at the avenger outside the gate.

The avenger gazed at me thwarted in its plan.
Raising its visor and wiping its eyes.
The avenger had no disguise - but only my face.

Under Cover

Wear a tin hat today. You need it!
You never know what is to be.
You cannot be prepared for the arrows of life.
Wear the hat. Push it on firmly.
Make your ears hurt and head throb.

Be prepared for danger, anger and the stormy blast.
Duck for cover, run and hide, peek over the wall.
Graze your knees falling to the higher place.
Flack and glass and bolts from the blue.
Dust and grime and grim reality watch for you.
Wear a tin hat today you need it.

You need protection. You need to be aware.
You need to cover your position. You need to hide.
The dust will never pass you by.
Rubble means trouble.
Trouble of the past.
Trouble to come.
The crater looms.
Is this the news today for you?
The red letter title shows the headlines of your life.
The black type smudges and marks your fingers.

You cannot live uncovered and unprotected.
You hang in the bunker. Breath gasping.
Eyes shut to the dust and debris.
Day after day you skid to a halt and dive for cover.
Wear a tin hat today. You need it.

What a headache. What an existence.
What a life. Get a life not just living hell.
By dying in fear each hour and minute.

Wear a tin hat today you need it.

Safe

Safe in his arms.
Safe in the arms of a father that really loves
That really cares.
That is not just a presence or a feeling but a real living being.
A person who weeps on your neck as he holds you.
A father that does not leave at the front door and –
- go to a distant land.
Abandoning you.
Abandoning you to the wolves and jackals.
The desert place with no water.

He is the father that brings cool water to your eyes.
Cool words to your heart and cool breath that brings life in the fiery place.
His arms are so strong and can reach as far as the end of the universe.

Don't push his searching hands aside.
He is marked on his palms with your name and date of birth.
With your birth certificate engraved on his brow of pain.

He has already suffered with you.
Just curl up close to him.
Just curl up and rest.
Rest not just for today but eternally.

Be safe!

Speed Trap

Diversion ahead. Bend in the road.
Mind the bumps. Ford ahead.
Signposts, signposts. This way. That way.
Red neon, silver bands, blue lights flashing.
Red and white taped boundaries.
Cones, cones and more cones.
Diversion ahead.
I want to put my foot down, speed ahead.

I'm late. I'm late. Bang the wheel.
Glare into the rear mirror, cluck your tongue.
Make obscenities to the anonymous driver.
Speed around the roundabout.
Pedal to the metal.
Through the floor, burning rubber.

Diversion ahead.
Screeching brakes, sideswipe the door.
Must hurry, must get there in time.
Green faces in the back seat.
The drivers having a bad day.

No games to distract the mind, you can't!
The road is too bumpy, hand clinging straps.
'Are we there yet!' echo's the mind.

Diversion ahead.
I know the way, clock ticking time away.
Reaching the known road the welcome street.

But NO lights on. No dog barking day.
NO welcome mat!

What day is it?

I thought it was Tuesday!

In a Spin.

What if my thoughts are true?
What if they come to pass and bite me.
What if the reality of fears burn me.

My mind is in turmoil. My emotions high.
I spin in this whirlpool of doubt, fear and pain.
Lurid visions of adultery, sickness, death are my companions.
I sit and talk to these visions in my mind.
Feeding them with more darkness and more death.

Spin round and round, get giddy, get in a fix.
My mind is bound to the path I have set it.
I have decided to think this way.
I have fed the soul with doubt and fear.
I have increased the vocabulary of destruction.
I have sought the lexicon and dictionary of doubt.

What if? What will happen, if this happens then what!
Round and round I spin.
A merry-go-round, a vertigo of darkness.

Light cant pierce there sides and come in.
The barrier is fixed and strong.
But I really wish I could get out of this trap.
This trap of imagination.
This trap of the empty mind.

Fill up my mind with something else is the whisper.
Fill up this little corner over here with hope.
With a little pool of cool love.
Fill up this little crack this little breach.
See it spread. See it water the parched mind.

Wash the dark corner of your mind.
Until you are flooded with the cleansing stream.
The clear thoughts that come from the pure mind.

The mind of purity of the God who reclaims you.
Cleanses you and waters you!

Flight Path

Baggage!

Heading for the exit. The way out.
The last stage of the journey.
The journey home.
The journey towards the light!
The light that has guided and gilded your life.
Baggage is on my shoulder soon to be shed.
Soon to let go and go on to the victory.
The end of the back breaking toil.
The bent neck and bent soul.
On towards the start of a new life.
Start of a new heart beat and new countenance.
New flesh. Young vibrant but helpless.
On to the new life bought by death.
That death the gateway beckons and waits.

The light is glorious to a point. To a star.
Feet stumble but keep going. The light waits.
A door is to the side open and welcoming.
A small straight door. A rest room. A side place.
But I go forward in my plan and foot fall.
Padding, plodding to my death.
I want to have a rest.
A venture to others peace.

I believe what I see.
I don't believe what's behind the welcoming door.
I don't check the name on the door.
The master of the room of rest.

'J. C.' sparkles on the paint shiny and new.
'J. C.' is above the blood red carpet.
The door knob is easy reach to let entrance
But I have the co-ordinates for my journey.
I will not turn aside.
The door is passed and groans in sorrow.
Creaking in pain for the lost one.
The key holder sighs but still waits for the next one.
The next soul on its journey.
Will you follow my path or the side door exit!
Choose before it's too late. Choose now

Why?

I had asked the question time and again.
Why did this happen, why does this occur.
I sought the answer in wise words and reason.
I sought the answers from holy ones and angels.
'Why' was a clarion call to my soul?

I was roused into action each day by this call.
The blessed in my ears shattered my thoughts.
My mind was full of reason and rhyme and truth.
The truth seemed to have a lot of sides.
The truth seemed to flicker and jump.
From teacher to teacher and rabbis knees.
Why, Why I asked!

The guru had a special answer whispered to me.
Whispered at a cost.
The 'why' grew too loud. Ear blasting.
Shaking my faith, my joy my peace.

The 'why' the answer I wanted -
would not come, no solution, no tuition.
It would not teach me a thing.
The search would have gone on forever.
Forever to the horizon of my strength and will.

But I stopped still in my tracks.
A sudden shuddering stop.
Heels burnt, toes dug in the ground.

Why do I want the answer to 'why'?
When the answer is 'Me'.
The 'Me, My and I AM of the universe.
'Why' lost its power.
Now was sought.
I was at the solutions source.
Satisfied but unfathomable.
At peace with the 'why'.

Why not you?

Clock Face

I cannot go through the next second.
It presses on me as a threat.
Pain - far too deep.

The next second is like a blanket of death and darkness.
"Lord I cannot live through the next second".

This is a real pain a reality for many souls.
The mind is crushed and destroyed.

Hear the voice again.

"I cannot go through the next second!
I cannot survive the torture it will bring.
The cry is heard by God himself.
His eyes weep and his arms reach out.
He whispers gently, "I am here in this next second.
I am your strength for the moment!"

Hear the voice again.

"I cannot go through the next minute".
The next minute is so painful and crushing.
The answer is the same for this cry, for this plea.

Help is there, is unseen perhaps unfelt.
But this help is as invisible as the atoms but more real than them.
Live through the next second even if you fear it.

He is your shepherd and your soul's friend.
The time will stretch and begin to grow for you.

He is your companion in 'time'.

The hands are blooded in love.

The face of the creator of time is marred.
He is gentle and does not speed up time.
He keeps pace with you, not hurrying.
No haste. He knows time heals.
Every second is his ownership.

Hear the voice again.

I cannot live the next hour. It is too painful.
But I have lived the last minute the last second.
I have survived even though I still suffer.

Go in trust back to the timekeeper.
He is not stressed that things are not hurrying.
He comes as a companion and healer.

Do not fear the condemnation of friends.
They have their own time frame.
They do not know what you are going through.

The hour soon becomes a day!

A day of hope.

The little gleam in a second has grown to a twenty four hour span.

His arms span eternity and also cuddles your heart.
He comes, and is in your mind and body and spirit.

Eternity is with you in every microsecond.

The atomic clock created will wind down.
But he is the caretaker of your soul and your time.
AMEN.

Shut it

Keep your mouth shut, button it.
Don't let your little tongue have a party.
Keep your mouth shut. shtŏom, shush, quit it!

The mind likes to hear its own voice and its opinions.
Keep it quiet!
Don't put your foot in it.

But I know what I think and feel I want to speak.
I want to show that I am a person of great thinking.
I have a lot of wisdom and study and knowledge.
Listen to me!

No keep it quiet, shtŏom, be at peace, careful.
I stood at the podium in front of my peers, one to one.
Whatever the ears listening to my words 'hear' is 'turned'.

I say it straight and clear but I don't think I don't reason.

I said keep it short, easy language any can understand.
I plugged my mouth in but forgot my reason and mind blanked.

It was blanketed in pride and passion and the pen.
It gave the speech eloquently and subtlety.

Everyone must understand everyone must agree now.
'Keep it quiet' the little voice in my mind tried to shout,

But I did not listen I was too clever.

My foot was in my mouth and I dug myself into the grave.
I should have kept quiet, I should have listened.

Oh dear!

Chatter

Invisible voices are moving in the air.
They chatter and clatter and find their rest.
Nobody knows who sends them or their source.
Are they the truth, are they a bending and a twist.

They are accompanied with images.
They dance and swirl and show wonders and horrors.
The invisible voices and their companion sights.
Bless some, lie to many and bend the mind.

The voices are sent over boundaries and reach any target -
willing to tune into or connect to.

The voices can be disguised in many forms.
Some speak like a child and wish to play.

But treachery lurks and darkness lies.
The little voice so innocent is from a brute base -
that knows no conscience.

How do we protect our ears?
How do we even protect our innocent ones?

First of all we switch off, we turn the knob.
We listen with a discerning heart.
We do not assume all is true but question it.
Protection from invisible foes and mind-bending words.

Be wise, ensure the transmission is true and clear.
Do not muffle your ears protect your eyes.
Tune in wisely. Ensure the signal is green.
But always remember the off switch.

Listen

Have you forgotten me? Have you lost my address?
You wanted to write to drop a line to communicate.
The list had been set before time itself.
I am not at the top in the 'A' section.

You have forgotten me. I am sure I never hear from you.
You go to another mentor another voice getting strength.
Getting requests answered.

You forgot me. I am standing here open hearted.
My voice has been silenced and overlooked.
You get no true answer no quick reply - no easy way.
You beat your chest and cut your face to get replied.

I am here I am standing in front of you.
I am invisible to you because you have forgotten.
You have forgotten that my sacrifice and death saved you.
It saved you from death and sin but also 'the struggle'.

You do not have to storm the gates of heaven!
You do not have to shout to the hills, to the pearly gates.
Tap me on the shoulder! I have been waiting patiently.

I turn my face to you and you see I have already been speaking.
I have already opened my mouth for you. I already pray.
I already intercede for you.

The blood from my hands is on my face.
I have cried for you, broke for you, spoke for you.

I am your interceder your in-between eternally.
Your permanent voice to the Father in heaven.

My name is Jesus!

Incoming Mail.

The finger is poised over the keyboard.
The hand had moved to and fro entering the promise.
I promise to send, I promise to give, I promise to take.
The finger was poised waiting for completion.
Waiting for the reply in the box.
The 'receiving mail' blinked and running.

Hope came in the heart of the operator.
The reply is coming, the answer the final piece.
The puzzle would only be completed with the last piece.
Be patient the answer is coming!

The screen moved and the answer came.
Shock went over the face of the operator.
It's a virus not an answer. Its darkness and not light.
The operator had not been replied too.
He moved closer to the screen waiting one more time.
Nothing moved on the screen. No incoming message.

The sender had not done the task allotted.
They had not given, not prayed, not loved, not been generous.
They had worried, plotted and murmured.
No answer will come they had cried. Nothing is real.

The operator had run out of time.
His finger hovered over the buttons.
He would not press 'enter' but 'Delete delete delete!'

The screen went blank.
No communication today. Empty air!

D E L E T E

Shorty!

"Jesus I need you!" I shouted at the top of my voice.
"Jesus I need you!" I shouted again till hoarse.
I was clinging onto the branches and flinging my arm.
"Jesus I need you!"

I was only a little man, so here I perched -
- up in the branches over people's heads-
- but unseen below.

Jesus was walking by and people were running.
Running ahead, beside, behind.
I was only a little man.
Overlooked unseen even hated.

I suppose hate is better than nothing.
But I hated hate. I did not thrive in destruction.
But I was a little man always overlooked.
I had talent. I loved my children - even my dog.
People even sneered at that.
I was a little man - a Jew overlooked.

I had plenty of money not always honestly gained.
The coins spilled out as I clung to the branches.
Eager beavers below scooped up - stilled - cheered.
They called "Jesus the healer is coming!
The preacher is here!"

I steadied myself and cried for the last time.
"Jesus!"
Just by his name.

He looked up - right into my eyes.
Piercing my soul with his gaze.

"I need you today!" he said this to a little man!

He still does. He still does today.

I Have a Cunning Plan

"I have a plan to take over the world!"
A gasp went out "The world! It's impossible, it's not reachable!"
They chatted to each other.
Then he said "Do you want it too?"
They nodded in agreement.
That little globe had already choked them.

The leader stood up and showed his plan.
They gazed in amazement as the simplest plan.
Stratagem was revealed.
"GIVE THEM WHAT THEY WANT!"
He shouted, "Give them all that they want and need and yearn for!"

But we are rich, so rich they replied. "We will become poor!"
"Oh no." said the leader. "The treasure is their souls!"
"The greatest prize.
The blue ribbon for all of us!"

They did not think of the cost again and stood in unison to praise.
They praised the leader till their hands hurt and throats dried.
They realized 'this plan' was so perfect nobody could spoil it.
They would get a thousand times more returns on the investment.
A million times more.

They emptied their pockets. Gold silver and jewels were showered.
They filled the barrels with many blessings.
They were overflowing, but they had more to give.

They pulled off their golden clothes and threw them in.
They ripped off their halos of light that crowned them.
They tore off the sandals of gold that protected them.

"We give all to you our leader and protector and saviour!"
"We give our blood and souls and beings to you!
Do what you will!"

"We praise and honour you above 'god the almighty!"
Princes and kings, emperors and tyrants, rich and -
paupers will praise you!
Oh Lucifer our divine leader!
Nothing will destroy you.
Nobody has your strength.
Not even one of those feeble mens' blood can destroy you!"

Star Bright

The stars foretold the birth of the king.
They moved into heavenly spaces showing the way.
They have no mind of their own but are pushed by Gods finger.
They shone, glowed and radiated the eternal plan.

Men gazed upwards looking for the portents and signs.
They trusted their gods but some knew the real truth.
The wise ones took the pattern as a revelation from heaven.
They packed their belongings, maps and instruments.
They rode weary miles towards the eastern sky
They gazed and wondered and began to praise when it stilled.

The silence grasped their souls as they entered Jerusalem.
To the great king, notorious and cruel they bowed.

"King tell us where we shall find the new king, the foretold one!"
Herod scratched his beard, smiled sweetly and gave the prophecy
"Bethlehem."
"Bring back news to me of the place of nativity!" He cried

To the little town they came, from kings directions.
They bowed their heads as they entered the place of birth.
The place of joy and pain - smells and light.
The place of poverty - humility.
The perfect place for a king.

They bowed their heads, removed their crowns and worshipped.
They worshipped the one that they had searched centuries for.
They worshipped the 'Eternal' in a fragile form.

A newborn child in mother's arms.

He was called "Emmanuel, Jesus and would be:
"The Christ"

Amen!

Study Guide

The student had studied through the night.
He had burned the midnight oil.
Words circled him.
His eyes were tired and his head ached.
He slowly slumped down to the realms of sleep.
He had studied well, absorbed all the written word.
He was a persistent studier. One day at a time.
He had dug deep, asked questions and believed.

His eyes were now in deep slumber.
Even there words, thoughts and truth circled him.
His dreams confirmed all he had read.

Dawn came over the windows edge.
The glorious sun woke him up gently.
The birds sung a song of awakening to his ears.
He woke refreshed. Ready to study a new day.

This day he studied the text while he worked.
While his hand busied himself working to live.
He supported his family - his mother and his sisters.

He studied even when he spoke to the neighbours.
Not one day was free from learning and seeking.
He had time for others – time for all.
He then became a teacher not the student.

Jesus was now the rabbi.
The one closely followed.
Even now he continued in 'the word'.
He spoke 'the word'.
HE IS THE WORD!
Amen.

Speak Up

I have been waiting here for many years.
My legs are useless, hang down weak.
I used to have close friends that helped me.
They now only bring me here, dump me and leave.

The years have spun on.
Sometimes I don't beg for alms.
Occasionally a holy man comes by and blesses me.
Sometimes with words but never with bread.

I sit in the sun because I cant move anymore.
The blessing comes once a year. A certainty.
A certainty of healing and recovery.
But I sit here hope gone, eyes now dark.

They said that a healer is coming this way.
A man of great love and compassion.
They say that he can heal ALL who call on his name.
They say that the 'Lord Most High' has blessed him.

I sit on my grubby mat thirsty and dry.
My legs have sores but I can't feel them.
I've been here for so many years, my back now breaks.
My heart has turned to dust. No hope anymore.

I don't lift my eyes when the stranger arrives.
He moves towards me. I don't even look up.
I have lost all hope, inclination and passion.
I lift my arms to my face and die.

The man moved to the fellow by my side.
He had called to him.

I was now quiet.

Judas

Black was the colour of his heart.
It had beat with light and life before -
the blackness oozed out of his pores.
Not a secret anymore.
The darkness had been seen by his friend.
No glimmer of light anymore.

The others in the group were colour blind.
They did not see into the heart of the traitor.

The 'black hearted one' lifted his face to greet.
To greet his greatest friend - mans enemy?
He felt the man was destroying hope of salvation.
He was not the 'saviour' expected.
He lifted his face kissed and greeted.
A sigh came from the man beloved but now despised.

Despised because he was not a warrior - a king.
Not as written and foretold.

But the black heart had not read the times.
He had not understood the true nature of the 'expected one'.
His heart had turned to stone and to death.
He had to ensure that the man would fight.

He kissed him to make him raise his arms.
To make him take up weapons of war.

But the arms had another purpose.
The arms of God are not used.
They are opened wide.
They are abused and they win!

Red

Paint him red. Don't leave a gap or a splash unfinished.
Paint him red. Unclean, blemished and vile.
Paint him red.

He is washed white and unscarred.
He is not marred with undeserved punishment.

What does your god look like?
Is he gold and silver?
Does he shine and sparkle and jingle in the pocket.
Does your god stay out off reach out of grasp?
Does your god move up and down with the promise of fortune.
Does your god say that everything is obtainable?

The real true god is painted red.
It is a danger sign, a flashing light a crossing place.
A place of choice. A place to be reckoned with.

Your god is held up high and seen by all but not recognized.
Your god crumbles and breaks into dust.
It is not as invulnerable as you thought. You are broke.

Paint him red the true god in the heavens.
The true one who allowed himself to be humbled.
Humbled beaten bruised for all to see.

Not a romantic picture. Not a love story.
But 'The love story!'
He was painted in red.
No other colour would do.
Admire his handiwork!

Royal

They covered him in purple. The most costly dye.
The most precious garment used in a base way.
The mocking was beginning.
The haunting of shame.

The thorny branch was twisted in pain on his face.
The branches broken, as his head, would snap.
The beginning of chastisement by another enemy.

He had already suffered at the hands of his kinsmen.
They had not acknowledged their king.
These enemies, strangers, gentiles - knew better.
They knew in there inmost that this was not a man.
They did not understand this knowledge.
They only saw a man ready for the whip.

They covered him in purple. A royal robe.
It was not covered in jewels but spots of blood.
It was not furred or adorned with braid.
It was covered in the spent body, the poured out flesh.

What a wonderful garment. What an enthronement.
Cast to the minions of a tyrant and flogged.
Nobody bowed in reality only mocking obeisance.
The crown was removed the robe discarded.
The nakedness was ready for clothing in a different pain.

I cannot cloth you in purple -
but I can clothe you in praise and glory!

O Happy Day!

I had a smug look on my face.
I had won. We had won!
No more Jesus!
No more 'king' talk.

It had been a busy time.
Celebrating the Passover.
Officiating in the ceremonies.

The lambs had been slaughtered.
The joy of Passover had been revealed.
It was a satisfying time.
Enemies obliterated.

He was not much of an enemy – but he was disposed of.
I feel really pleased.
The sun shines on the righteous.

I have a model, in gold, of David's harp.
Even the strings work.
Exquisite workmanship.
David was my hero.
A man who wanted the temple so much!
The 'house of God' bought into existence.

I picked up the little memento. It was so beautiful.
I placed it in direct sunlight and enjoyed the 'glow'.
I chuckled. My heart felt like that little glow.
Total bliss. Total peace and joy.

'What is that noise? – spoiling my contemplation.
My 'me time'.

"Jonathan! See what the noise is about!
I am in the 'Presence of the Lord'!
I must not be disturbed".
Jonathan left.
Peace reigned in my heart.
All's well with the world
My world!
A new and peaceful day waits!

C.E.O.

I was told you were in charge.
In charge of everything.
You were the ultimate authority and governor.
I had put all my faith and hope in who you are.
The chief of all, the head of the company.
You have set all the rules all the systems to live.

I had come to your office many times with petitions but no entry.

Can you supply my needs and my wants today?
Can you move others to do the right thing for me?
Can you set boundaries for all to make us successful?

The company motto 'ALL in control' was burned into us.
YOU are 'all in control' so that is why I am here.

I found myself today at the back of the queue.
Petitioners and workers were gathered before me.

The door was opened and closed in rhythm.
All comings and goings properly timed.
My turn came.

As I neared the doorway the motto 'All in control' was on the plaque.
It was so familiar that I was encouraged to enter.

I pulled out my list of complaints, petitions and needs.
All carefully typed and justified and categorized.
I pushed towards your chair ready to plead.

Nobody was there!

I was stunned.
The motto on the desk said 'I will be back soon.
I'm already defending your cause.

I AM in control when you ask for me!'

160

Opinionated.

Don't put words in my mouth.
'I never said that! I never thought that!'
Don't put your opinions on my words.

Why do you slant and slander and twist my words?
You need to find the truth that I say clearly.
You need to, but don't want to.
You hide behind your intelligence and opinion.
You slant my words to your view and outlook.

It's not me who hides. It's not me who shies away.
You put a bucket on your head and try to speak.
You ensure that your words are heard.
You protect yourself from truth.
Because you only hear the echo you believe it.

I never said these things that shake you.
My eyebrows were never contorted in false anger.
I did not do the things that dreaming opinions say.

My life has been an open book of truth of many years.
My words, actions and thoughts infinitely examined.
Yet you still follow the tramline, the rail track.
You will not even glance to one side and think.

It's so sad that truth stands before you but you are blind.
You are deaf to the truth. Blind to the light.
Move one step sideways. If you really want to seek me!

Books, pamphlets, films and video clips show reality!
Really do they? Do they say the truth or opinions?
Seek out the truth. The real truth. The real ME!

You will find it if you really seek it.
You will find that truth is staring you in the face.

I ALWAYS HAVE!

The Easter Egg

The perfect design holds life in its bounds
It was laid to give life.
All that is needed for life is encased here.
You cannot fall or be destroyed by yourself.
You can only be destroyed by the cruel one.
The one who smashes life to pieces and laughs.
You were designed to receive life.
All the good sustaining things that make you grow.
It may not be obtainable by your sight.
But look carefully, go inside, be sustained and revived.
You are safe here. Pressures push in at all sides
You are safe here.
I designed this place.
My hands moulded and shaped it.
My hands lifted it up and saw light through its edge.
It is so fragile and sometimes you forget and are broken.
The dream of a new life runs out.
But don't forget I am the creator not the destroyer.
Life, new life is in me for ever.

You cannot destroy me.
This symbol of my sacrifice.
This symbol of resurrection.
This symbol of unity under pressure.
This symbol of togetherness.

This symbol is a pale copy of reality.
This symbol rolls in my hands, never lost.
My scarred hands that made the egg
Made a way for eternity in you.
Made a way for existence in me.
Made you my child to be!
Life in eternity today!

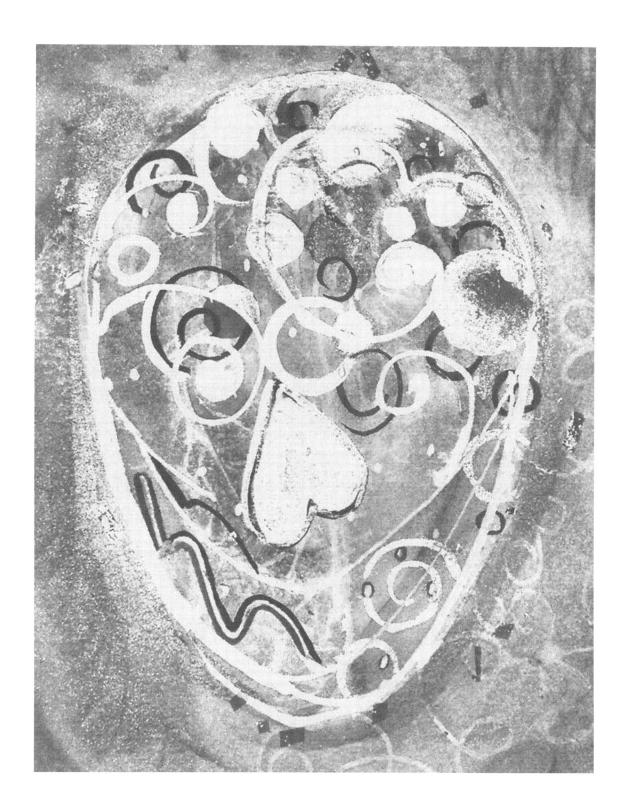

Reservation

"Step to the left please!" Your place is waiting.
Your reservation space is ready just for you.
All is prepared ahead of you, just as you ordered it.

You wanted a private place where all needs were met.
A place of sanctuary and sanctity an eternal abode.
All is ready all is waiting.

"Step to the left please".
The stairways on your side.
The door is ready and swings open as you reach it.
"Step to the left please!"

The light blinks above the door - 'No exit' flashes.
It connects to the beat of your heart, you begin to fear.

"Step to the left please!"
You begin to panic it does not seem right or correct.
It does not seem a peaceful eternal entrance.
The light hits your face. 'vacant and ready' it flashes.
You grasp the handle all anticipation has fled.
"Step to the left please!"
Others are now pushing behind you.
A great crowd follows.
Step to the left.
Time has finished, close the book.
This message shines in your eyes as through the portal you go.
"Step to the left please."
"I don't want to go!" you cry.

But too late the door is shut!

Trumpet Blast.

"Blow the shofar. Purse your lips and praise him.
Lift your heads into the air as brothers.
You have been brought at a price and redeemed."

The shofar is blown a thrill goes through the crowd.
Jews and Gentiles.
Arabs and Negroes.
Caucasians and Orientals.
No race is out of earshot.

The light is pouring into the streets of Jerusalem.
It falls from the sky and bathes and burns the stones.
Hearts have been bruised, horded sin 'beaten' again.

The hearts beat with a dancing tune.
Hands multicoloured grasped each other.
They spin in circles and made patterns of joy with their feet.
The nations were drawn to the eternal city.

His nations composed of Abraham's seed and offspring
Were all gathered as a unity.
No cells divided or poisoned.
They just grew in love for him and each other.

The shofar was blown until glory fell.
All bowed into the sand of Jerusalem, of New York of Moscow.

All heads 'crowned' by him bowed.
They bowed on this final day.
They had no sin at all.
Light burned out the darkness.
The darkness went to its place.
The gates of hell opened.
The nations were split into sheep and goats.

The harvest was gathered.

The seed had grown.

The 'Word' gathered his glory in his arms, and took them home!

Study 39
113 Cash in your Chips.

Life's a gamble. My ship is coming in. Alls well that ends well. How much energy do we use to gain something that appears fantastic? We strive to get the second car the second home but we can only live in one at a time. The cost of these spares can be too high to pay. The credit card is cut in half. Unusable. Not just the card!

Study 40
121 Mosaic. 125 Body Image. 150 Shorty. 126 Cheap Cheep.

Even the smallest atom in the universe is huge in Gods sight. He created it. Gilded its shell. He values the least. He is rich in his infinite details. The smallest is never off the scale. The scale tips his way. Nothing is cheap or throw-away. Nothing is disposable.

Study 41
160 C.E.O.

We sometimes have to repeat a request because the listener appears to be deaf to out requests. We try all sorts of means to plead our case, e-mails, letters, and memos and eventually in person. We don't always get an answer straight away so we assume we are being ignored. Not always so! When you were last ignored how did you finally get the message through? I suppose the last question is 'what is the answer back!'

Study 42
117 Money Management. 118 Buy Me! 134 Who!

There are many bargains about and many fraudulent buys. Three for two when you really only want one item. All sorts of ploys to get your money or your soul! What are you prepared to pay and what is the true cost?

Study 43
147 Chatter.

We are affected by everything we encounter, ingest or see in the world from the media, other people, sites and sounds and much more. We many times deny any effect at all, we are untouched, unmoved and still the same. Or we can be over cautious and never connect because of fear that we will be affected. Or we can be too open and in naivety accept everything at face value. A good idea to read between the lines and not sign on the dotted line without reading the small print. What do you read in the wee small hours? What is your bedtime reading? Check it out and then see what sort of day you had today.

Study 44
152 I Have a Cunning Plan.

We all have plans. We have big dreams but perhaps small purses. Are our plans foolproof with no holes or traps? You may plan to build a tower and raise a roof but have you been raised! You can't raise enough money to pay for your soul your destiny Not just God has paid the price. Others have an interest in you. Others have used all there finances to purchase you. Their accounts are emptied making room for you!! What is the number on your account. Are you numbered in the Lambs book of life! Or does another signatory have you on his books.

Study 45
136 The Avenger. 132 Point of Contact.

Who of us is running from something or someone? The foe may be imagined or real. Who really knows? The breath is hot on your neck. Fear is also an enemy that slows us down. Can you really be free? One person you will never be free of is yourself. Do you like yourself? Is your true foe you! What strategy do you use to escape? What is the correct answer to your permanent dilemma? What is the destination you are going towards? Where do you find safety?

Study 46
159 O Happy Day.

You've read the end of the book. You have sussed out 'who done it' 'who got the girl' before the ending was revealed. You enjoyed the conclusion and were satisfied. What if the writer had a different idea than you? What if tragedy turned out to be a triumph? What if you were not the winner but did not know till the last page.

Study 47
116 Late Bloom.

You've always fallen behind everyone else. Always second best. Others have always been cleverer, prettier, richer more talented. They have been recognised, praised and useful. You are in the shadows. Each plant, each tree had season and a pattern of growth, maturity and fruitfulness. It is built in and fits each plant with the surrounding world perfectly. Not too early not too late. Don't suppose that you are a dead stump in the ground. Look green shoots appear. It was not to be in spring but a late harvest is waiting for you to enjoy and for the world to gather and relish.

Study 48
149 Incoming Mail

Writing a letter and getting a reply is a dying art. E-mails are the fashion. Quick speedy requests and answers flash before your eyes. Suppose you are not connected, your payment to the server is overdue. You stare at the blank screen wondering why no reply. You sent correspondence, the prayer, the request. What interrupted, intercepted the transmission? What got on the wire before you and cut it!

Study 49
154 Study Guide.

What you walk in you get soaked in. If mud you get dirty. If water you get clean. What time and space do you allow for the living word. The 'living Word' that is not just a cold figure on the page but a reality a creative being. Words of hope give hope. Words of love give love.
A transmission from God that you can tune into at any time.

Study 50
124 Pride and Prejudice.

Do you get your self image from your peers or from the TV in the corner? What makes you different? Do you follow the crowd? What personality do you look up to and emulate. Who do you like to be a copy of? Are you a clone of the world or a unique reflection of Jesus Christ? Clones have a built in flaw of destruction. Love the only means to copy accurately. He could not shout any louder. His voice was hoarse. Stopped by darkness. But His voice continues even when und heard by human ears. His message and plead goes directly to the throne and the ears of His Father.

Study 51
135 Limping Legs.

Such a short time to succeed. Only a few opportunities left. Ok push others aside make way for me. Rush, rush, rush. What is the result can you be certain of, you will succeed. Be first. 'Hard luck to the weak' your motto. The strong rules OK.

Study 52
114 Embryo.

From tiny acorns great oaks grow. A little idea too small to be noticed by the big boys. Down in the deep dark earth. Even the smallest has the largest potential. Even losers of the race will win the prize. Life can be good!

Study 51
158 Royal.

'Clothes maketh the man' a popular saying. What we wear is a reflection of who we are. Sometimes though clothes are forced on us. The convict, the patient, the older person. They have to succumb to another's choice. Their true identity is then lost in the crowd. All dressed the same. One was forced to wear a poor imitation of a stately robe but it was transformed before their eyes into an eternal robe true in form, identity and meaning forever.

Study 52
155 Speak Up

Patience is a virtue Time and tide wait for no man. The time is right. Strike while the iron is hot. All immediate sayings. What if you don't notice the time you are in. What if the seconds go too quickly? You cannot get lost time back. Speak up now! It may be the last chance. Don't forget though there are soothsayers and prognosticators that tell you the 'times' that we are in. Read the book that has the beginning of time and the end of time already written in it. Don't rely on all timekeepers. Rely on the one who made time for us.

Study 53
115 The Stain.

Things can get too big to conquer. Too large to knock down, overcome or to complete. Do you have short arms or short of time? Use what you have. Don't get overwhelmed. Get support by those who are stronger than you. Don't get yourself stuck in a corner or in a rut because of fear or failure. A little at a time. You will complete the task with time to spare.

Study 54
164 Reservation. 137 Under Cover .131 Battle of Words.

There are times when people are called to war. We live in a time of great dangers. These are times when the call is broadcast aloud for the departure of train or plane. People rush all over the place criss-crossing the globe. Many never talk or mix with the other travellers. In their own little world. A time will come when only a few will be going the same way as you. Who is going the correct direction? When do you depart? Perhaps its now! What is your protection and your guide for the fight not just for now but also tomorrow.

Study 55
139 Speed Trap. 146 Shut it..

We all have plans and plots for the day. Often things go wrong from bad planning. We know it's wrong or sloppy but forge ahead. Do you listen to the still small voice that tells you how to do this or that? Or do you have deaf ears even to your own common self to save face. Or are you just stubborn. Up a blind alley no way out. Trapped because of yourself! Who has never had a day when everything is a rush? We leave everything to the last minute. The rush and hurry inevitably leads to something important being forgotten. Diaries and calendars are very useful but we never know which one is our last page. You are not the only one infected by this hurry sickness. Perhaps this will make you think about your time span, your eternal soul. Did you forget about it! Put a note down "action for today". Today he will hear your voice tomorrow you may be silent.

Study 56
157 Red.

The costliest gift ever given has everlasting life as the prize. The cost paid in a fragile man of flesh but with heavenly origin. Encapsulated and fixed in time. The perfect plan incarnated. The symbol of death hangs around necks but this symbol of new life is consumed. Think about it.

Study 57
128 Face 2 Face.

We all have an image of ourselves in our mind. Some of it is constructed by ourselves some is painted by others. We get an idea we can never do something because of something or some view of ourselves. No one is insignificant all can be useful. All are beautiful!

Study 59
157 Red.

Many artworks of Jesus have been sanitized and cleaned up. A beautiful clean and colourful portrait. We forget that he lived in a dusty hot country. He was marred with the hard life that he chose. He used and moulded wood to his pattern. He suffered jeering from his family and friends. At the end he was not a pretty site but a face and body not recognisable anymore. He peered through swollen eyes and was not suntanned anymore but blood covered. Red is his robe and his badge. He chose this way of portraying himself and his heart. He dipped his finger in the pot of the world and painted! The portrait of God.

Study 60
138 Safe.

Fathers are supposed to be comforting safe. Tragically not all fathers are! The race of men can change but they are flawed. They are marred with sin. We all have a father that cannot change and is not flawed! We gaze on perfection but see imperfection because we have been damaged too much. Our identity has been burnished by pain into a mirror that does not know see the truth. The truth even hurts our soul but the truth made the light and the reflections. He will and can make your vision of him and of yourself be perfect. He has set this down in his flesh that all will be healed and restored. Lift up your eyes.

Study 61
144/5 Clock Face.

There are many kinds of punishment that can be mans lot. You could get locked away, isolated, tortured. One of the worst is to live with all the memories of the bad things that have happened. The good things remembered would be overcome, overshadowed by the bad. What if we could never be healed from bad memories? What if we could not escape from the past? This is one way of facing the next minute. Remember that you are not alone the memories you feel both good and bad are remembered by the one who came to heal and to make new everything. You are not alone. He can reshape your mind into one like his. Remember he has forgotten your sin!

Study 62
148 Listen.

He could not shout any louder. His voice was hoarse. Stopped by darkness. But his voice continues even when unheard by human ears. His message and plead goes directly to the throne and the ears of his father.

Study 63
156 Judas.

Black is usually portrayed as an evil colour. Natural black is made up of all the colours of the universe! Black can be a jet gem, coal that brings warmth and light. It's the colour of many innocents put to slavery. Rise above colour blindness. Don't judge by the outside it's the inside that counts. Some hearts are the colour black. They can be accepted by everyone but death is inside. What type of hear have you?

172